Medieval Decorative Art
JOHN CHERRY

Published for
The Trustees of the British Museum by
BRITISH MUSEUM PRESS

© 1991 The Trustees of the
British Museum

ISBN 0-7141-2065-0

Published by
British Museum Press,
a division of
British Museum Publications Ltd,
46 Bloomsbury Street,
London WC1B 3QQ

Designed by Roger Davies
Phototypeset in Photina by
Southern Positives
and Negatives (SPAN),
Lingfield, Surrey
Origination by Colourscan,
Singapore
Printed in Hong Kong

BELOW The gittern, a plucked musical instrument, elaborately carved from boxwood. The head and neck are formed in the shape of the body of a dragon, and the sides have decoratively carved panels. English, early fourteenth century.

Contents

Introduction

Medieval secular art often survives only in fragmentary form; it is frequently difficult to find, and hence it is often ignored. Another reason for its relative neglect was the dominant role of the medieval Church. Throughout the Middle Ages the Church was the chief patron of the arts, and an enormous amount of money was spent on the decoration of buildings and the provision of objects for worship in order to illustrate and glorify sacred belief and history. The resurgence of interest in the Middle Ages during the nineteenth century – the Gothic revival – was inspired by both the Romantic movement and the growth of religious feeling; the religious aspects of medieval art were therefore stressed more strongly.

Secular art probably measured less, both in quality and quantity, than religious art. It is not easy to judge the accuracy of this statement, however, since secular art has been damaged far more by the effects of change and time. A great deal was executed in perishable textiles such as linen or tapestry and decorated with embroidery; some was painted on wall plaster; some was enamelled or engraved on gold or silver that might be melted down in times of crisis. Churches and monasteries, despite the Reformation, have not suffered in the same way as secular palaces, castles, and town and manor houses, which have been repeatedly altered, rebuilt or destroyed. Religious art has often found a safe haven in churches, while secular art has not been afforded the same protection. Secular manuscripts of the Middle Ages have survived better, however, and literary scholars have examined the illustration of secular romances and, in the case of the Arthurian cycle of romances, the influence of such illustration on tapestries and objects.

Nevertheless secular medieval art, particularly on objects, remains neglected. To provide an introduction to the subject – which undoubtedly warrants a more detailed and thorough treatment than is possible here – I have chosen to concentrate on four themes; each provided an inspiration for the production and decoration of objects. Of course, other themes might have been chosen instead of or in addition to these four, and all could be treated at greater length in a longer book.

Despite the growth of urban life in the twelfth and thirteenth centuries, the population of medieval Europe was dependent for its survival on agriculture, which has been described as that 'perennial war between man and nature'. Thus the natural world, its foliage and animals, and the labours of agriculture feature in the decoration of objects.

Heraldry was invented in the Middle Ages – its symbols and colours made it attractive to those who wished to display their position in society or proclaim their ownership of objects. Heraldic devices were often displayed at feasts, festive occasions for entertainment as well as for eating, but a variety of other influences also affected the uses, shapes and decoration of the vessels and implements used. Finally, courtly love, a new phenomenon of the twelfth century, provided a theme which underlies both the illustration of medieval romances and the decoration of the rings and jewellery often exchanged as gifts between lovers.

Roger Sherman Loomis, the great American authority on Arthurian literature and legend, drew attention to the presence of an unusual design at the beginning of Richard de Fournival's *Bestiaire d'Amour* (Bestiary of Love). This shows a strange tower with a double entrance: one door is decorated with a human eye, the other with a human ear. Richard explains that his book is concerned with the nature of beasts and birds, better realised when painted than described. Through the two doors of the eye and ear enter all the knowledge kept in the memory; to understand the past, the imagination needs both verbal and visual assistance. In this sense I hope that the words, photographs and drawings in this book will together begin to reveal the fascination of medieval secular art.

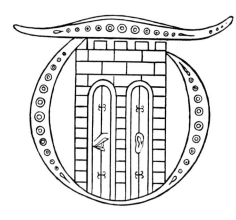

1 Design from Richard de Fournival's *Bestiaire d'Amour*.

1 Nature and rural life

In the Middle Ages agriculture was fundamental to most other human activities. Good harvests were essential not only for the peasants but also for the survival of that tiny minority of rulers, priests, nobles, merchants and artists who were responsible for the objects described in this book. The natural world of plants and animals is reflected in the decoration of medieval objects, most usually in a stylised manner. In the thirteenth century a new realism emerged in the depiction of foliage and animals.

In illuminated manuscripts, scenes of rural life were depicted in calendar illustrations of the seasonal activities proper for each month. In the classical world, such representations were more often shown as passive symbols than the active work favoured in the Middle Ages. The types of activity considered appropriate for each time of the year became known as the Labours of the Months.

Just as agriculture can be seen as part of the conflict with nature, so also can the struggle with animals. One of the principal forms of rural recreation was hunting: in this activity the king and noble classes could demonstrate their energy, skill in understanding the lie of the land, and their nobility. In the later Middle Ages an increasing interest in flowers and gardens reveals a new approach to nature. Nobles and lovers were often portrayed in secluded gardens, and it may be that this seclusion marks the increasing social division between those who enjoy, however briefly, the beauties of the flowers and those who labour to produce them.

The combination of animal and foliage motifs has a long history; it was a major theme of decoration in the Anglo-Saxon period. An eleventh-century ivory pen case is carved with pairs of birds and beasts placed symmetrically on each side of a central foliate stem, from which issue fronds of acanthus foliage entwining animals. Indeed, the antecedents of

2 Birds and beasts entwined in a foliage scroll on the top of a late eleventh-century ivory pen case.

3 Stylised 'stiff-leaf' foliage surrounding the body of a griffin on a thirteenth-century bronze mould from Hartlepool, England.

this kind of inhabited foliage can be traced back to classical sources. In the Middle Ages, however, there was greater variety in the ornamental treatment of foliage and animals. For instance, a major shift occurred in the thirteenth century, when the depiction of foliage, animals and the human form became more naturalistic. This new approach in some cases depended on a closer observation of nature. Villard de Honnecourt, an early thirteenth-century master architect known today from a remarkable sketch-book in the Bibliothèque Nationale in Paris, drew a lion and wrote of the picture, 'Know well that this was drawn from life.' Even though his drawing of the lion is in fact rather conventional, Villard's remark echoes the view of the thirteenth-century philosopher, St Thomas Aquinas, that art is an imitation of nature.

The change from a stiff, formal foliage decoration to a more naturalistic depiction of leaves can be seen most clearly today on stone sculpture, particularly on capitals in churches. This transformation becomes apparent in the first half of the thirteenth century

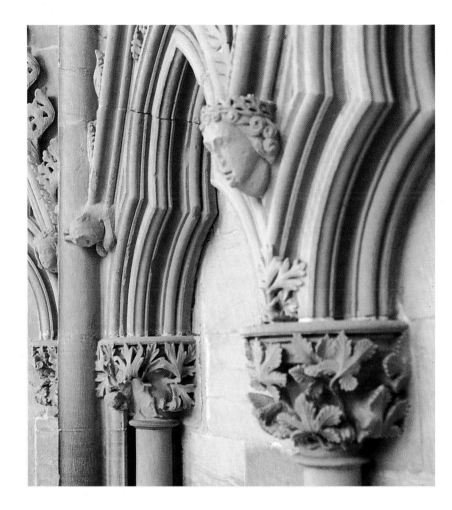

4 (*Left*) Naturalistic leaves and dragon in gilt bronze on a crosier attributed to a mid thirteenth-century goldsmith from the region of the River Meuse, Belgium.

5 (*Above*) Naturalistic foliage on late thirteenth-century capitals in the chapter house at Southwell Minster, Nottinghamshire.

in France, most notably at the cathedral church of Rheims. The older, more stylised form of foliage may be seen around the griffin on a bronze mould from Hartlepool. Here, ₃ stylised leaves and fruit issuing from the mouth of the lion beneath the griffin form a decorative background. This may be compared with the more naturalistic foliage, particularly the vine leaves, on the crosier probably ₄ made by a goldsmith in the Meuse valley in the second quarter of the thirteenth century.

The change from what has been called 'stiff leaf' foliage to more naturalistic foliage also appears in England in the thirteenth century. The building of Westminster Abbey under the patronage of Henry III (1216–72) in the 1240s and 1250s as the burial and coronation church of the kings of England gave the opportunity for the introduction of naturalistic foliage decoration from France to England. It may be seen on the wall arcades of the ambulatory chapels and the transepts of the church. In England this development reached its climax in the sculptural decoration of the chapter house of the minster church at South- ₅ well in Nottinghamshire, dated to the 1290s. Here there is a dazzling array of leaves of vine, oak, maple, buttercup, hop, bryony, ivy, hawthorn and rose.

The remarkable medieval gittern is an ex- contents page cellent illustration of the use of foliage and animals as decorative motifs. A gittern is a plucked musical instrument and forerunner of the modern guitar. The style of the carving dates it to the early fourteenth century. Carved from a single piece of boxwood, it is shaped as a monstrous dragon with scaly wings, green eyes, claws and a fearsome mouth. The body of the dragon flows into a series of stems of vine leaves which spring off from the finger-hole of the gittern. The sides of the gittern are divided into panels of naturalistic foliage of vine leaves, hawthorn and oak leaves in which people hunt or animals play. The intricate

detail makes this a virtuoso example of wood carving.

The gittern could have been played with other instruments such as a fiddle, harp, portative organ or trumpet, but its most frequent use was to accompany songs. Unfortunately, the great lack of surviving English secular music from the fourteenth century means that we do not know exactly what might have been performed on the gittern during the first period of its existence. We do know that songs were often of love or the seasons and sometimes combined the two themes. The opening lines of the poem 'Alison' (c.1300) shows the association of love and spring:

> Betwene Mersh and Averil
> When spray beginneth to springe,
> The lutel foul hath hire will
> On hire lud to singe.
> Ich libbe in love-longinge
> For semlokest of alle thinge –
> He may me blisse bringe:
> Ich am in hire baundoun.

(Between March and April/when the twigs come into leaf,/the little bird has her wish/and sings with her voice./I live longing with love/for the fairest of all –/she may bring me happiness;/I am in her power.)

The oak leaves and acorns on the gittern are clearly shown in a natural manner, yet their size is enormously exaggerated; some of the acorns are almost half the size of the pigs. The main scene on the left-hand side of the gittern shows a man dressed as a peasant using a long pole to knock ripe acorns off an oak tree to feed the pigs below. In calendar illustrations in medieval manuscripts, feeding pigs was often depicted as the appropriate Labour of the Month for October or November, fattening up the animals for winter slaughter. The late medieval Scottish poet Gavin Douglas reflects the autumnal fattening of the pig in these lines:

> ... fat swyne in sty
> Sustenyt war by mannys governance
> On hervist and on symmeris purvyance.

(Fat pigs in the sty/were sustained by man's management/of the harvest and the fruits of the summer.)

The December scene in calendars often represents the killing of the pig for Christmas.

It is not surprising that the decoration of the panels on the gittern relates to the scenes of the Labours of the Months. The framework was ultimately derived from Roman calendars, preserved for us in the calendar illustrations of illuminated manuscripts, as well as in major sculptural programmes on the façades and around the porches of the great French cathedrals such as Amiens or Chartres.

Little remains to us of the decoration of the palaces of Henry III (1216–72), but the Labours of the Months were important among the secular images used to decorate them. They were painted on the side of the chimney of the King's Chamber in his palace at Kennington, south of London, in 1265 and were on the hood of the fireplace in the Queen's Chamber at Clarendon, near Salisbury, Wiltshire, in 1251. A similar series decorated the fireplace in the Painted Chamber at Westminster, which was one of the most important parts of the palace in the time of Henry III. Here there was the figure of Winter, which is described as being by 'its sad look and miserable portrayal of the body likened to Winter itself'.

One of the few surviving images of the Labours of the Months is in the remarkable series of wall paintings of c.1330 at Longthorpe Tower in Cambridgeshire. This almost complete survival of a medieval secular wall-painting scheme is unique in England. The

7 Weeding, the Labour of the Month for June, as shown on a late thirteenth-century tile from Chertsey Abbey, Surrey.

tower was added *c.*1300–10 to an earlier house and was probably built by Robert de Thorpe (d.1329); the paintings were executed either for him or for his son Robert. January is depicted holding a bowl of soup and warming himself at a fire.

Series of Labours of the Months also occur on the decoration of medieval tiles. The medieval tiles with secular subjects found in the nineteenth century at the Benedictine abbey of Chertsey in Surrey were probably initially designed for one of the royal palaces of Henry III such as Winchester or Westminster. The scenes were depicted on roundels. All are fragmentary, but the most complete in the series is Weeding, a scene usually assigned to June or July. Here a labourer, tunic tucked up and tied at the knees, uses a weeding hook and stick. The series was probably repeated on different floors and perhaps in different buildings.

Such repetition is clearly illustrated by the lead roundel, which has a miscellany of six scenes of Labours arranged in no particular order. They are Pruning (February or March), Hawking (May), Reaping (July), Threshing (September), Sowing (March or April) and, in the middle, Killing Pigs (December). The roundel was cast in a mould and therefore no doubt a considerable number were produced, prob-

ably to decorate caskets. This shows how a series of subjects used for the decoration of royal palaces could also be represented on more everyday objects.

Gaston, Count of Foix, a Pyrenean nobleman of the late fourteenth century, epitomised the occupations of the knightly class in the Middle Ages as war, love and the chase. Hunting was supposed to have an ennobling effect on those who pursued it, and conversely adroitness and skill were the mark of a noble person. In the romances of Tristram (see p.56) his skill in cutting up a stag so impresses the huntsmen he meets that he is taken to the court of their king.

All forms of hunting had merits: game might be stalked on foot; approached in a camouflaged cart; driven into traps, pits, enclosures or nets; or killed with falcons. But the noblest and best form of hunting was the chase of the deer with running or scenting hounds. To do this a huntsman would first select a suitable deer to hunt, then return to his hounds and divide them into groups stationed along the predicted path of the deer. The stag would then be raised and the hunt commenced with the huntsmen on horseback. The same stag would be pursued and each group of hounds released as the stag passed. The mid thirteenth-century seal of Simon de Montfort, Second Earl of Leicester illustrates this form of hunting. It shows him blowing a horn while galloping across a hilly mound, with hound beneath. After a successful kill the body of the stag was dismembered.

Hunting was not a purely masculine activity. The enamelled sides of the mid fourteenth-century King John cup, from King's Lynn, Norfolk, shows elegantly dressed men and women engaged in hawking and hunting. There are twelve women (one holding a long bow, and two holding hawks), nine men (one about to blow a horn), and animals including hares, hawks and a fox.

8 Warming by the fire, the Labour of the Month for January, as shown on the wall-painting on the west wall of the Great Chamber at Longthorpe, Cambridgeshire. Early fourteenth century.

9 (*Right*) Six Labours of the Months, shown on a lead roundel which may have decorated a thirteenth-century English casket.

10 (*Far right*) The seal of Simon de Montfort, Second Earl of Leicester, attached to a charter dated 1258, shows him hunting with his dog.

contents page
6

Hunting occurs repeatedly on the panels on the sides of the gittern. To the side of the finger-hole the huntsman aims at the stag with a crossbow while others set free the dogs and blow horns. On the other side of the gittern, the depiction of a man chopping at an oak tree may be part of a fox-hunting scene, since there is a fox perched in the branches of the tree. This interpretation is supported by the adjacent illustration of fox hunting, where a huntsman is about to unleash a dog to catch a fox eating berries, while from another angle a man and pack of five hounds approach, hunting the fox. These scenes on the gittern stress the huntsmen, providing a contrast with those on the Savernake horn where greater prominence is given to the animals used for hunting and to their prey.

The Savernake horn was carved in the twelfth or thirteenth centuries out of elephant ivory and mounted with enamelled silver bands in the fourteenth century. It was preserved as the forest horn of the Wardens of Savernake Forest, in Wiltshire, from the late Middle Ages. English forests and the animals in them were protected by royal laws from the time of the Norman Conquest, and hunting in them was the prerogative of kings and magnates or of those clerics who had forests. Richard FitzNigel said that the forests were the kings' chambers and their chief delights, for kings came there, laying aside their cares now and then, to hunt as a rest and a recreation. The importance of this royal restriction of rights is demonstrated by the decoration of the Savernake horn: on the topmost band is a formal scene of agreement between a king and a bishop; a forester stands on one side with staff and horn.

The decoration on the two topmost bands of the Savernake horn is divided into sixteen compartments. In addition to the people mentioned above, they show alternate figures of hunting dogs and various forest animals. The dogs and animals are reserved in gilded silver against a background of green and blue translucent enamel representing the forest. The range of forest animals shown is very wide since it includes, as well as hart and hind, a squirrel, lion and even a unicorn. The fore-

11 Carving on the medieval gittern (see contents page), showing a man chopping a branch from an oak tree. He is in pursuit of the fox who has taken refuge in the tree. The adjacent scene running up the right-hand side shows a man about to unleash a dog to hunt a fox who is eating berries.

most place on the lower band, beneath the lion, is occupied by the stag with its horns; it also stands next to the lion on the upper band. This prominent position reflects the importance of hunting the stag.

Falconry, the pursuit of game with hawks, is also represented on the Savernake horn. On the rim around the mouth of the horn are no less than sixteen trefoil arches which enclose

hawks preening their wings and breasts and flapping their wings. Hawking was indeed a favourite sport of kings and nobles. Frederic II, Emperor of the Holy Roman Empire (d. 1250), wrote a treatise on the art of hunting with birds (*De arte venandi cum avibus*).

Falconry was also particularly associated with noble ladies. The late thirteenth-century seal of Isabella of Sevorc, a noble lady who

12 (*Above left*) Hawks preening themselves on the rim of the silver band around the mouth of the Savernake horn.

13 (*Left*) The two silver bands added to the Savernake horn in the mid fourteenth century show a king and bishop conferring while a forester attends; beneath are the animals of the forest. The horn was associated with the forest of Savernake in Wiltshire from the fourteenth century.

14 (*Above*) The bands on the Savernake horn also show (*top, from left*) a hound, stag and seated lion, and on the lower band a fox, hound and stag.

15 Elizabeth of Sevorc, a noble lady of northern France, shown riding side-saddle with her hawk. Her seal matrix is printed in reverse so that the inscription can be easily read. Late thirteenth or early fourteenth century.

16 Birds, berries and leaves in a drawing of the lost decoration on the Coronation chair in Westminster Abbey, painted by Master Walter, the King's painter, in the winter of 1300.

lived at Sebourg near Valenciennes in northern France, shows her riding side-saddle holding in her gloved right hand a hawk attached by its jesses, the thin straps which were released when the hawk was thrown into the air. In her left hand she holds an enormous claw, probably a badge of the family. The imagery of hawking was also carried over into the world of love (see p.66), where it acquired a symbolic significance.

Birds were used as decoration on a wide range of secular objects. They may be seen on the Coronation chair in Westminster Abbey. This chair, which was used in the centre of the sanctuary for the sacramental aspect of the coronation, was built at the order of Edward I to house the stone of Scone captured from the Scots in 1296. It was made under the direction of the King's painter, Master Walter of Durham, in 1300–01. The enthroned King, symbolising the King's presence, was formerly represented on the inside of the back, with his foot on a lion. The inside of each arm was decorated with birds among oak foliage. The hawk was also used as a decorative motif. The copper-alloy mould from London for hammering out spangles (dress decorations in copper alloy or silver) shows a number of birds including a cock, a hawk with outstretched wings and an elegant crowned hawk with long tail and floating scroll issuing from its mouth. In the mould this is not inscribed, but an inscription would no doubt have been added later.

The struggle between man and animals was also a favourite theme in art. Combats with animals occur on seals and tiles. The tiles from Chertsey Abbey contain a series of combats between men, between knights and lions and tigers, and between men and animals. One of the most impressive of these tiles shows a youth clad in a tunic who spears a lion through the back of the neck while his hunting dog runs beneath, a design that may have

inside back cover

17 Birds, faces, a squirrel, and the wheel of fortune on a cast from a fourteenth-century copper-alloy mould, found in London, for producing brooches and dress fittings.

been derived from a classical scene of a lion hunt.

One of the main sources of inspiration for the portrayal of animals was the medieval Bestiary, a collection of descriptions of birds and beasts, often illustrated, to which Christian moral and allegorical interpretations were given. The lion was regarded as the embodiment of strength, 'leo fortis' (the strong lion), as well as being associated with images of kingship and nobility. On the Coronation 16 chair in Westminster Abbey the King was shown seated with his foot on a lion, and the

seated lion on the Savernake horn may be 14 associated with the royal ownership of forests. In the stories of Reynard the Fox it is the lion who is king, and on seals the lion is often referred to as the King of the Beasts. Since the lion was supposed, according to the legends in the Bestiary, to sleep with his eyes open, many seals show lions curled up asleep at the base of a tree, with the surrounding legend in English: 'wake me, no man'.

The lion was a real animal. Unicorns and griffins were mythical animals, but in medieval treasuries the claws of griffins (in reality the horns of rhinoceros or wild goats) were preserved. Griffins were thought to have the wings and head of an eagle attached to the body of a lion. Lions are sometimes used decoratively with griffins, as on the pavement of the Queen's Chamber at Clarendon Palace 18 where they face each other. The decorative use of the griffin is shown on the copper-alloy mould from Hartlepool used for the production 3 of silver or lead roundels which would have been used to decorate caskets.

Parts of different animals were combined to produce grotesque creatures (for instance, a bird with a human head) which were another favourite motif for decoration. On a piece of leather armour for the upper arm found in 19 London, the decoration tooled in low relief consists of grotesque birds and beasts encircled in foliage with three-pointed leaves. Some of the two-legged creatures have the body of a bird and a man's head; others have the body of an animal and the head of a dog, bear or bird.

In contrast to ferocious or monstrous animals there were those with a more domestic or playful significance. Dogs and cats were kept as pets. The noble in the tapestry from the Cluny Museum is about to knock the bone 24 away from his dog. Devotion to animals is revealed by the representation of dogs on tombs, such as those under the feet of the two wives of Robert Braunche of King's Lynn. The 47

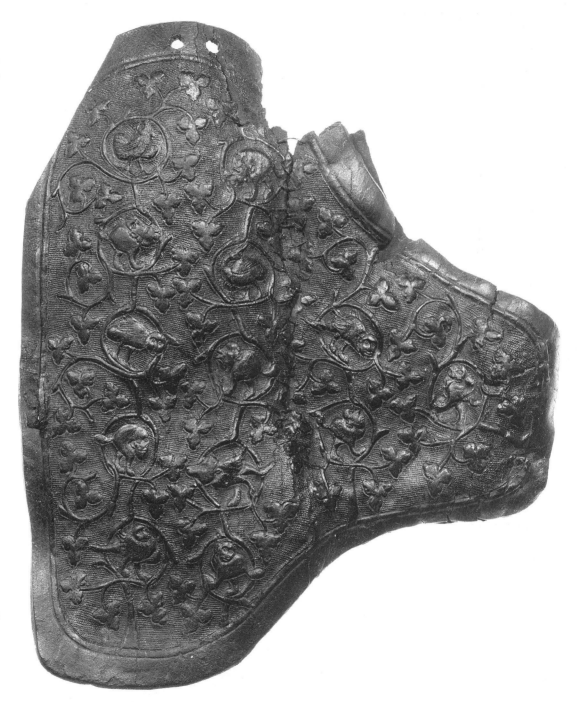

18 (*Left*) Opposed lions and griffins from the inlaid tiles in the floor of the chamber block built for Queen Philippa at the royal palace of Clarendon, near Salisbury in Wiltshire, 1251–2.

19 (*Right*) Birds and monstrous bipeds, some with human heads and others with animal heads, arranged amidst foliage on a piece of early fourteenth-century leather armour for the right upper arm, found in London.

dog was traditionally seen as a symbol of faithfulness and loyalty. The story of King Garamantes, in the medieval Bestiary, tells how he was captured and sold into slavery, but 200 of his hounds formed a party to find him and rescued him from his enemies, fighting those who resisted.

The monkey or ape (babewyn) was the most playful animal, whose antics gave rise to the term babuinare (to paint marginal figures of animals in manuscripts) derived from the Italian word *babuino* (baboon). Babewyns are characteristic of the reign of Edward II (1307–27), appearing not only in manuscripts but also on pottery. Walter Skirlawe, Bishop of Durham (1388–1405), had a great silver-gilt cup, enamelled with babewyns and a knop (knob) which was in the form of a bird's nest with three men climbing up to steal the young birds. The silver plate of Edward III (1327–77) included a ewer with a monkey playing a harp, a hanap (cup) with swans and ladies bathing, a ewer with children riding pick-a-back, and a cup with babewynerie.

The ape was sometimes shown parodying the actions of humans. He could even defend the Castle of Love (see p.63) against attackers. Another example on a tile from Malmesbury Abbey depicts a monkey parodying a physician examining urine in a flask, probably intended as a satirical comment on medieval doctors.

Animals were used to illustrate both the medieval attitude to hierarchy, with the noble lion as King of the Beasts, and also the reversal of the idea of hierarchy – the world turned upside down. In this world oxen slaughter butchers, hares roast their hunters and boil their hounds. The story of Reynard the Fox is full of this type of reversal, where the cunning fox is defeated by his natural enemies. Geese will hang or ride him, hens will barbecue him. In one tile the timid hare or rabbit is shown blowing his trumpet while riding on the back of a hound.

20 A drawing in a Bestiary produced around 1200–1210, showing King Garamantes led away into captivity and subsequently rescued by his dogs.

During the fourteenth century a more idealised attitude to life in the countryside seems to have developed, particularly at court. An early example of this in decorative art is a red velvet cap embroidered with pigs eating acorns in a flowery meadow under the trees: this was listed as a purchase in the French royal accounts for 1352. Pastoral scenes were clearly a favourite subject with Louis of Anjou, whose inventories of 1403 record a set of green hangings embroidered with shepherds and shepherdesses eating nuts and berries. He also had a cup enamelled with shepherdesses playing the bagpipes, wearing mantles of gold and blue and hats of different fashions, and holding their dogs by silver cords.

Tapestries were expensive and were used by nobles to decorate their halls and principal reception rooms. Sometimes they depicted romances and heroes, occasionally scenes of peasant life. Such rural scenes are shown on a

23 tapestry made in Tournai c.1460–70 and now in the Burrell Collection, Glasgow: it portrays both men and women preparing for a rabbit hunt by taking a ferret from its box, laying nets over the rabbit holes and holding dogs on a leash.

Enclosed gardens became part of the graceful aristocratic life in the late fourteenth and fifteenth centuries. The walled castle garden, laid out with rose trellises and arbours, plots of herbs and banks for repose, provided a scene for peace and romance. The appeal of gardens and flowers is shown by another tapestry

24 where a noble and his lady stand in front of a tent set amidst flowers. The lady sprinkles water on the flowers in the container beside her, while the noble uses his stick to play with his dog.

An idealised attitude to the natural world appears to have been common among nobles in France in the early fifteenth century. The idyllic view of the peasant is shown on a

25 leather sheath made to hold a set of carving knives. The four knives, two large and two small (see p.41), all have the arms of John the Fearless, Duke of Burgundy from 1404 to 1419, and are the earliest in a group of late medieval enamelled knives bearing the arms of the Dukes of Burgundy and their leading followers. The arms upon the shields of these knives indicate that the knives were made for John the Fearless between 1385 and 1404, before he succeeded his father, Philip the Bold, as Duke of Burgundy.

The sheath enables us to follow the history of the knives after they passed out of the possession of the original owner. The letters Y and O on the right-hand side of the top of the sheath are the initials of Ysabel, John's

21 (*Above*) Drawing of a fourteenth-century tile showing a hare riding on a hound.

22 (*Above*) Drawing of the design on a fourteenth-century tile showing a monkey examining urine in the manner of a medieval physician. The tile was found at Malmesbury Abbey, Wiltshire.

23 (*Left*)
Peasants hunting
rabbits with
ferrets and nets,
on a Franco-
Burgundian
tapestry of about
1460–70.

24 (*Right*)
A noble with dog
and a lady with
watering pot
watering flowers,
on a mid
fifteenth-century
tapestry woven
in France.

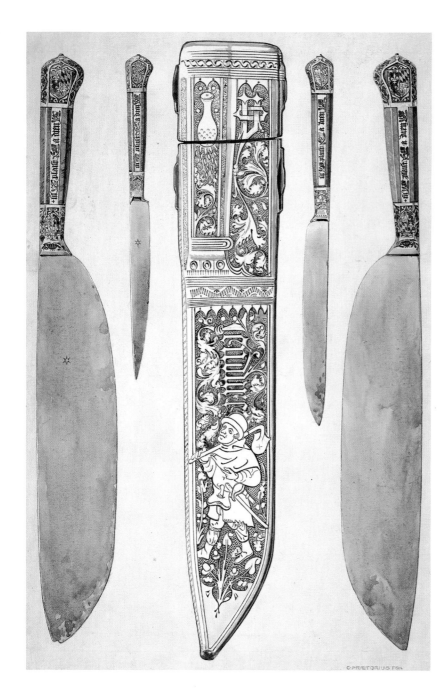

25 A watercolour of the sheath and set of four knives that belonged to John the Fearless, Duke of Burgundy, and subsequently to his daughter Ysabel. The knives are Burgundian, late fourteenth century and the sheath French, early fifteenth century.

daughter, and of her husband, Olivier of Blois, Count of Penthièvre, whom she married in 1406. John presumably gave the knives to his daughter, perhaps on the occasion of her wedding. Opposite the initials is a watering pot, a vessel with a single hole at the top and many holes at the bottom, which was filled by immersion. Its contents were first retained by the vacuum created by closing the hole at the top, then released by opening it. The falling water made the watering pot an appropriate symbol of mourning, and it was used in this way in the early fifteenth century. Since Ysabel died in 1412 at the early age of twelve years, the sheath must have been made for Olivier shortly after Ysabel's death. The peasant on the lower part of the sheath is shown walking to the fields in his rustic clothes with tools such as his hoe over his shoulder. He makes the comment, 'J'endure' (I go on), a motto which can be interpreted in at least two ways. It may contrast the age of the peasant with the youth of the dead Ysabel, or it may be comparing in an ironic and bitter manner the everyday continuity of agricultural existence with the frailty of aristocratic life.

In using the pastoral theme as a comment on the brevity of aristocratic and the length of peasant life, the craftsman who produced the elaborate decoration of this sheath for a nobleman may be underlining the dependence of the whole of medieval society on the successful outcome of the struggle against nature. However, it was the struggle of man against man that produced heraldry.

2 Heraldry as decoration

Heraldic decoration pervaded much of daily life in the medieval period. It was used not only by knights in tournaments and battle but was an important element in all manner of ornament. Shields of arms decorated the walls and windows of buildings, the sails of ships and the harness of horses, and were to be found on objects ranging from weights to leather scabbards to domestic plate and caskets, and even on the vestments and liturgical vessels used in churches and monasteries. In an age less literate than ours, the widespread use of such devices had a greater practical significance than may be apparent to us today.

Heraldry

The development of heraldry, the systematic use of hereditary devices, is a feature of the twelfth century. The evidence of seals shows the use of heraldic devices in France, England and Germany as early as the second quarter of the century. These devices can be definitely described as heraldic because they are inherited by the next descendants of those who first bore the arms. By the beginning of the thirteenth century heraldry had grown into a symbolic and pictorial language with its own system and classification.

The decorative use of devices or patterns may be seen on the shields of the knights on the late eleventh-century Bayeux Tapestry or on those of the ivory chessmen found on the Isle of Lewis in the mid twelfth century. The knight shown here has a cross on the upper part of his shield.

The horse was essential to the mounted knight, so it is not surprising that heraldic decoration quickly spread from the shield to the trappings of the horse. An impressive example of the use of heraldry in this way is on the seal matrix of Robert Fitzwalter (d.1235), which shows one of the leading barons of the early thirteenth century. He gallops across the seal with his sword raised, a dragon cowering

26 The shield on this knight, from the mid twelfth-century walrus ivory chessmen found on the Isle of Lewis in Scotland, shows the use of a simple decorative pattern.

27 (*Above*) Fragment of silk applied work with embroidery showing the arms of Albemarle on either side of the arms of Rivers. English, between 1248 and 1260.

28 These four copper-alloy heraldic pendants show the royal arms of England (*above*), Richard of Cornwall (*above left*), the family of De Bohun (*far left*), and the family of the Valence earls of Pembroke (*left*).

beneath. The arms of Fitzwalter are shown both on his shield (held in front) and on the trappings of the horse (before and behind the rider). Robert Fitzwalter was one of the leaders in the barons' revolt against King John (1199–1216) which culminated in the signature of Magna Carta by the King in 1215. He was also one of the twenty-five barons who were to see that the provisions of the charter were carried out.

In front of the galloping Robert on the seal, another shield shows different arms – those of the Quincy family, whose leading member at this time was Saher de Quincy (d.1219), a political ally of Robert Fitzwalter. They served together in the campaigns in Normandy which led to the loss of the duchy to the English Crown after the Battle of Bouvines in July 1214. Indeed, their experience in Normandy may have set them against King John. Matthew Paris, a chronicler at the Benedictine abbey of St Albans, Hertfordshire, wrote later in the thirteenth century that King John particularly loathed three men – Archbishop Stephen Langton, Saher de Quincy and Robert Fitzwalter. The political and military comradeship between the two may be indicated by the sharing of their arms, which occurs on Saher de Quincy's seal as well as on that of Robert Fitzwalter.

The spread of heraldry to minor parts of the equestrian equipment of the knight is demonstrated by the survival of large numbers of shield-shaped heraldic pendants. These small enamelled shields would have decorated either the breast band of the horse or the fitting on the headstall. The pendants show the arms of the kings of England, of Richard of Cornwall 28 (the brother of Henry III), the family of De Bohun, and the family of the Valence earls of Pembroke. The occurrence of the arms of Richard of Cornwall suggests that these pendants began to be used by the mid thirteenth century. They continued to be popular into the

pudore : ꞇ opeuantur ſieut diploide
confuſione ſua
Coufitebor domino nimis in
ore meo : et in medio multorum
laudabo eum
Qui aſtitit a dextris pauperis :
ut ſaluam faceret a perſequentibʒ
animam meam.
Gloria patri
Dñs Galfridus louterell me fieri
fecit

fifteenth century. The arms on the Valence pendant are very similar in their style of enamelling to those on the effigy of William of Valence (d. 1296) in Westminster Abbey.

On other seals heraldry appears on the knight's standard, on his saddle or on his surcoat. A surviving piece of linen with appliqué silk cloth and embroidery, of unknown use, shows the shields of the Rivers and Albemarle families. Therefore it is likely to have been made for William de Fortibus, Third Earl of Albemarle, who in 1248 married Isabel, sister and heir of Baldwin de Rivers, Earl of Devon. William died in 1260. Whatever the original object of which this formed

part, its survival was ensured by the fact that it was reused as a protective seal bag for an impression of the great seal of Henry III.

The spread of heraldic decoration to all parts of the equipment of the knight and his horse is shown by the illustration of Sir Geoffrey Luttrell being armed for a tournament. This is from the Luttrell psalter, a manuscript commissioned by Sir Geoffrey himself between 1320 and 1340. The arms of Luttrell are shown on his surcoat and ailettes (shoulder pieces) and on the fan-shaped crest and chanfron (headpiece) of his horse, as well as on both the back and the front of his saddle and the trapper (covering) of his horse. They occur on

30 Richard I kills Saladin by knocking him from his horse with a lance. These mid thirteenth-century inlaid mosaic tiles, found at Chertsey Abbey, were probably designed for a royal palace, perhaps Westminster.

the triangular pennon on the lance and the fan-shaped crest of the helmet handed to him by his wife, Agnes Sutton, and on the shield held by his daughter-in-law, Beatrice Scroope. Both ladies are dressed in gowns bearing on one side the arms of their husbands and on the other those of their fathers. This illumination marks the complete heraldic coverage of the knight, his horse and his ladies.

The arms that appear most frequently on the decoration of objects are the royal arms of the kings of England. These arms, three gold leopards – heraldically, 'three lions *or* (gold) passant guardant' – were first used by King Richard I (1189–99). They appear on his great seal, engraved in 1198 after his return from captivity after the Third Crusade. King Richard is shown in combat with Saladin on the floor tiles from Chertsey Abbey that were made in the thirteenth century. The design on the tiles shows Richard with a crown on his helmet and, in his left hand, a shield showing the heads of three lions.

The three lions of England, used by the kings of England from 1198 to 1340, were not only shown on their shields and buildings, but also, from the second half of the thirteenth century, were widely used on objects ranging from the heraldic pendants that would have adorned the horses of messengers to the weights and customs seals used in the regulation of trade. The seal for Lincoln engraved in the reign of Edward I (1272–1307) clearly shows this use of the royal arms.

The complexities of royal heraldry at this time are shown by a little silver-gilt casket or chrismatory (container for holy oils) that has six shields engraved within quatrefoils on the lid. On the back are the arms of the kings of England dimidiated (cut in half) with, on the other half, those of the kings of France, azure (blue) powdered with golden fleurs-de-lis. These are the arms of Margaret, second wife of Edward I, who was a French princess. On the front of the lid are the same arms, with a label across both shields (a label is a narrow stripe across the top of a shield, with three tags or pieces hanging from it to distinguish the next generation). These arms belonged to Isabella, daughter of Philip IV of France (1285–1314). She was betrothed in 1303 to Prince Edward (later to become Edward II). The Anglo-French heraldry of the casket thus indicates that it could have been a gift from

31 Casts of the double seal for the delivery of Wool and Hides for Lincoln in the reign of Edward I (1272–1307).

Margaret to Isabella on the occasion of her betrothal.

The first major change in the royal arms of England occurred in 1340, when Edward III (1327–77) quartered the English and French royal arms. It was through the marriage of Isabella to Edward II, of which the casket is such a vivid reminder, that their son, Edward III, derived his claim to the French throne. In 1328, on the death of Charles IV, the last French king of the Capetian family, Edward III was the nearest male heir. However, his claim was through his mother Isabella, while the law of France forbade the crown to descend through a woman; the French barons therefore supported the rival claim of Philip of

Valois, who was crowned as Philip VI in 1328. Edward III formally claimed the French throne in 1336 and, to emphasise his claim, in 1340 he quartered the arms of France with those of England. This arrangement of arms can be seen on the half-florin or leopard of Edward III, struck at London in 1344: the obverse has a crowned leopard with a banner bearing the arms of France and England attached to its neck. This use of the crowned leopard is paralleled by the inscription on the tomb of Edward III in Westminster Abbey, where he is described as '*invictus pardus*' (the unconquered leopard).

The quartered royal arms assumed by Edward in 1340 may also be seen on a lead

33 This gold coin, a half florin of Edward III struck in 1344, has a crowned leopard with a banner bearing the arms of England and France attached to his neck.

34 Bronze seal matrix of Richard, Duke of Gloucester, later Richard III (1483–5), as Admiral for Dorset and Somerset.

badge associated with his son, the Black Prince (d.1376), and on the Ashanti ewer, and the back of the Wilton diptych (see p.33), both associated with Edward III's grandson, Richard II (1377–99).

The second major change in the royal arms took place between October 1406 and August 1408, when Henry IV (1399–1413) had a new Great Seal engraved. On this the simpler version of the French royal arms was used in the first and fourth quarterings. This version has three fleurs-de-lis and is known as France modern, as opposed to France ancient, which had a larger number of fleurs-de-lis. This new version can be seen on the seal of Richard, Duke of Gloucester, as Admiral for Dorset and Somerset, where they appear (differenced by a label) on both the sail of the ship and on the

35 The Valence casket, decorated with enamelled heraldry. French (Limoges) or English, early fourteenth century.

37

35

37 (*Above*) The heraldry on the hilt of this late fifteenth-century Sword of State indicates that it belonged to a Prince of Wales, either Edward, son of Edward IV, or Edward, son of Richard III.

36 (*Left*) Silver lid of a cup decorated with enamelled arms suggesting that it was a gift from Philip IV of France to Raoul de Nesle. Paris, *c.*1300.

banner at the stern. The Duke became King Richard III of England (1483–5) on the death of Edward IV (1461–83). The royal arms with France modern also occur on the hilt of the Sword of State of the Prince of Wales, where they appear on the shield held by two angels. The combination of the arms on both sides of this hilt, including those of Wales and Cornwall, suggests that the sword belonged either to Edward's son Edward, one of the princes who died in the Tower, or to Edward the son of Richard III, who died in 1484. His father's death in the Battle of Bosworth Field a year later brought the new Tudor dynasty to the throne with the accession of Henry VII.

Colour is an important element in heraldry. The main colours used in heraldic decoration are red, blue, green, purple and black. The use of *or* (gold) or *argent* (silver), the two 'metals', with a colour was preferred for brilliancy of effect to the use of either a colour with a colour or a metal with a metal. Two colours or two metals are only rarely found together or superimposed.

In metalwork the techniques of gilding, silvering and enamelling provided easy vehicles for displaying the different heraldic metals and colours. Indeed, from the fifteenth century the French word *émail* (enamel) also means heraldic tincture. The use of enamel on heraldic pendants has already been noted (see p.24).

The Valence casket in the Victoria and Albert Museum in London provides an excellent example of the use of enamel to demonstrate heraldic colours. It is covered on all four sides and the top with a diamond pattern of shields, almost as if copied from a large hanging. There are six shields on the casket. In addition to the arms of Valence and of England, it displays the arms of Brittany (Dreux), Angoûlème, Lacy and Brabant. The inclusion of the arms of Brabant and Brittany may indicate that it was made after two marriages:

of Margaret, daughter of Edward I, to John, Duke of Brabant, in 1290; and of Beatrice, sister of Edward I, to John of Dreux, Duke of Brittany, in 1305. Henry Lacy, last Earl of Lincoln, died in 1312. These marriages and the death of the Earl suggest a date for the casket of between 1305 and 1312. If so, the arms of Valence are those of Aymer, Earl of Pembroke (d.1324), the son of William de Valence (d.1296), whose wooden effigy decorated by the Limoges enamel workshops is in Westminster Abbey. On the casket the red and blue colours of the enamel are a particularly striking achievement of the enameller's art, and the lion of the earls of Lincoln is a subtle combination of blue and red to produce murrey (purple-red). The casket was probably intended to hold valuables and would have been lined with wood or fabric.

Another illustration of the use of enamel to provide heraldic colour is the lid from the cup preserved in All Souls College, Oxford. Here the 36 heraldry is shown in panels of champlevé enamel on silver divided by panels of cloisonné enamel, called in contemporary inventories *émail de plique*. In this rare technique the cloisons (cells) are formed from wafer-thin gold strips laid on the surface of the gold base plate to form a flower filled with opaque enamel colours; the backgrounds are in translucent green. The principal panel of champlevé enamel at the front shows the arms of France ancient and Navarre, and must be for Philip IV of France (1285–1314). The side panels bear the arms of Hainault and those of Clermont-Nesle; they can refer only to Raoul de Nesle, Constable of France, who married Isabella of Hainault in 1297. The original cup, of which only the lid survives, was probably a gift from Philip IV to Raoul de Nesle on the occasion of his marriage to Isabella.

Badges

A badge is a distinctive device or emblem assumed as a mark of recognition by an individual or family and often used as a mark of allegiance. Badges, sometimes known as impresses or signs, were frequently used in the late fourteenth and fifteenth centuries as shields became less easily recognised because of their quartering and subdivision. A badge was usually used alone and, unlike a crest, was not associated with the shield. Many of the reasons for the choice of badges and the occasions for their use remain unknown. That they became fashionable at the court of Edward III (1327–77) is, however, certain: he was particularly devoted to chivalry and heraldry.

In 1348 Edward founded the Order of the Garter, a group of twenty-four knights chosen by the King. Each had a particular regalia of which the most important part was the Garter. This was not a badge but was used to encircle the arms of the knight. The earliest known illustration of the Garter is on a lead badge commemorative of the Black Prince (d.1376), the eldest son of Edward III. On this badge he kneels before the Holy Trinity with his gauntlets on the ground in front of him, while his helmet is presented to him by an angel. The whole scene is enclosed by a buckled band inscribed with the Garter motto 'hony soyt ke mal y pense' (shame to him who evil thinks). A cloud overlaps the upper part, from which appears an angel holding the Prince's shield of arms. This bears France and England ancient with a label, and the same arms are repeated on his tunic.

One of the best-known badges is the feathers of the Black Prince. The badge of the feather was probably first used by his mother, Queen Philippa of Hainault, who owned plate decorated with black ostrich feathers. On the Black Prince's tomb at Canterbury, his arms alternate with a black shield on which are set three silver ostrich feathers, each transfixing a scroll with the words 'ich diene' (I serve). The sons and grandsons of Queen Philippa bore

38 (*Below left*) Drawing of a lead badge showing the Black Prince kneeling before the Trinity. Late fourteenth century.

39 (*Below right*) The White Hart badge of Richard II (1377–99) engraved on his quadrant.

40 (*Opposite top*) The Dunstable Swan Jewel. *c.*1400.

41 (*Opposite below*) The back of the Wilton diptych, painted at the end of the fourteenth century, shows the arms of Edward the Confessor impaled with those of Richard II and, on the other panel, his badge of the White Hart.

ostrich feathers with various devices. It is clear that the use of this particular badge was hereditary.

Another famous badge is the white hart of Richard II (1377–99), son of the Black Prince. According to contemporary inventories he owned jewels in the form of a white hart, and the badge was used on a wide variety of his possessions. Two that are illustrated here are the quadrant, an instrument for measuring the altitude of the sun or stars to determine the time, and the bronze ewer found at Ashanti (see p.50).

The hart badge may have been derived from the white hind borne by Richard's relation Thomas Holand, Earl of Kent. The badge also appears on the back of the Wilton diptych, a panel painting in the National Gallery in London, and here announces, with the clarity of a luggage label, the identity of the royal owner. The hart lies on rosemary; his neck is encircled with a collar in the form of a coronet, from which hangs a chain. On the other side the arms of Edward the Confessor are impaled with those of Richard II. Inside the diptych Richard is presented by his three patrons to the Virgin Mary. He is wearing his badge of the white hart and so are all the angels attendant on the Virgin. The way in which the harts are painted indicates that the chain falls from the coronet downwards between their front legs. They are clearly of gold, modelled in the round, and encrusted in the round with white enamel.

This enamelling technique was popular in Paris around 1400. An example of its use for a badge is the Dunstable Swan Jewel, a small piece modelled in gold in the form of a lively swan with one raised leg and beak slightly open. The gold has been modelled in imitation of feathers and the whole bird covered in white enamel to give the effect of plumage. Just as the white hart was the badge of Richard II, so the swan was the badge of the house of Lancaster.

It was used in the fourteenth century by a number of English families such as the de Bohuns, who were proud of their descent from the Swan Knight of courtly romance (see p.62). The marriage in 1380 of Mary, a Bohun heiress, to Henry of Lancaster, later Henry IV (1399–1413), brought the use of the badge to the Lancastrian royal house.

Some badges took the form of a rebus, a device forming a visual pun on a surname. This tradition probably originated in the canting or allusive heraldry of the thirteenth century, such as the trumpets of the Trumpingtons or the hammers (*martels* in French) of the Martels. A punning badge is the talbot (a type of dog, now extinct) used by the Talbot family, earls of Shrewsbury. A lead badge of a dog with the word 'talbot' written across the collar would probably have been worn by a retainer or supporter of the family. Such badges were particularly popular in the fifteenth century during the Wars of the Roses.

The political poems of the period often refer to people by their badges. John Talbot, Earl of Shrewsbury, was held a prisoner in France between October 1449 and July 1453 and a popular poem lamenting the English disasters in France refers to him by his badge:

> And he is bownden that oure dore shulde kepe
> That is Talbott our goode dogge.

(And the guard of our door is chained up/that is Talbott 'our goode dogge'.)

Curious objects were sometimes used as badges. On a fifteenth-century panel with the arms and the crest of Sir William Belknap, which originally hung in the church of Burton Dassett in Warwickshire, his shield is hung from a burning beacon. Beacons were often used as badges by admirals, but there seems to be no reason to associate Sir William with the sea.

Badges were used, like heraldry, to decorate

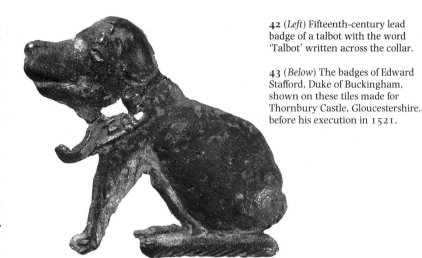

42 (*Left*) Fifteenth-century lead badge of a talbot with the word 'Talbot' written across the collar.

43 (*Below*) The badges of Edward Stafford, Duke of Buckingham, shown on these tiles made for Thornbury Castle, Gloucestershire, before his execution in 1521.

the possessions of their owners. A fine display of badges occurs on tiles made for the floors of the elaborate castle built for Edward Stafford, Duke 43 of Buckingham, at Thornbury in Gloucestershire in the second decade of the sixteenth century. Stafford was executed for treason in 1521 and his castle was left unfinished. The tiles show the royal arms in a bordure (heraldic border on the shield) with antelopes supporting the shield, all surrounded by the Garter. In the corners are four badges: the swan (a device popular with the Staffords), the flaming axle for Woodstock, the mantle of Brecknock and the Stafford knot. Here he is using badges to indicate his family descent and the lands over which he had control.

As heraldry became increasingly complex with more quarterings and the greater use of supporting animals and crests, badges became a simpler and more direct means of identification. They never supplanted heraldry but were used in addition to it, as the tiles from Thornbury demonstrate so well. Both heraldry and badges were employed to assert possession as well as status. This dual function at the end of the Middle Ages is well expressed in Shakespeare's play *Richard II*, when Henry of Lancaster accuses Richard II's henchmen, Bushey and Green, of crimes, saying that they had:

> From my own windows torn my household coat,
> Raz'd out my impress, leaving me no sign
> Save men's opinions and my living blood
> To show the world I am a gentleman.

44 Wooden panel showing the shield of Sir William Belknap hanging from a burning beacon. The panel was painted in the fifteenth century and originally hung in the church of Burton Dassett in Warwickshire.

3 Feasting

Heraldic shields or paintings of them were sometimes used to decorate the halls in which dinners and feasts took place. Eating is such a basic activity that it is worth considering how it was portrayed as well as the form and decoration of the vessels and utensils used in both cooking and eating.

Medieval representations of feasting cannot be taken as simple illustrations of what actually happened. They are interpretations, through the eye of the engraver or illuminator, of whatever the patron wanted shown. The depiction of the feast with which John, King of Portugal (1379–88), entertained John of Gaunt (1340–99) in 1387 was illuminated in a history written in the late fifteenth century and it therefore shows fashions of that date rather than of the time of the feast itself. Status was often emphasised in the placing of the guests. Here the King of Portugal sits directly in front of the fireplace with John of Gaunt on his right. A nobleman, an archbishop and three bishops make up the rest of the company. The portrayal of the feast shows a whole range of activity, from the cook ladling food from a three-legged handled cooking pot on to six metal dishes, to the squires carrying the food to the table. Here the diners are seated with their knives, trenchers, rolls of bread and three salts (see p.38) in the form of small circular metal containers with spiral decoration on the lids.

This royal feast may be compared with a less grand but equally informative picture of medieval feasting that occurs in the Luttrell psalter. This illuminated manuscript of the early fourteenth century, commissioned by Sir Geoffrey Luttrell (see p.26), a Lincolnshire

45 A late fifteenth-century illumination showing King John of Portugal entertaining John of Gaunt in 1387.

46 Sir Geoffrey Luttrell, shown in the Luttrell psalter, at dinner with his wife, two Dominican friars, and other members of his family.

country gentleman, shows scenes of everyday life and rural activities on his estate. In the dining scene he is depicted sitting at the centre of the table, with his wife and two Dominican friars on his right and other members of his family on his left. Sir Geoffrey's wealth and status are emphasised by the blue hanging, decorated with the birds from the Luttrell arms in silver, which covers the wall behind the table.

The table marks the distinction between those who feast and those who serve. A bearded servant brings two dishes and a cupbearer, his towel around his neck, kneels on the near side of the trestle table, having just given Sir Geoffrey his cup. The eating implements and drinking vessels are not placed regularly on the table as in modern place settings. Rectangular trenchers of bread are positioned in front of some of the diners, and the large flat dish in the centre of the near side contains further slices of bread. The shapes of the knives and spoons are clearly shown. Some of the diners are drinking from bowls, while Sir Geoffrey is drinking from a beaker. The vessels on the table were probably made of wood or silver, and the covered bowl near the cupbearer may represent a salt. It is noticeable that there are no jugs on the table; the large jugs that are such a feature of medieval pottery may have been used for serving rather than as containers set out on the table.

This domestic meal may be contrasted with the depiction of the Peacock Feast on the memorial brass of Robert Braunche, a rich 47 merchant and citizen of King's Lynn, Norfolk, who died in 1364. On this very splendid occasion the lords and ladies dine at a long

47 The Peacock Feast depicted on the memorial brass of Robert Braunche at St Margaret's Church, Kings Lynn, Norfolk.

table, while peacocks are brought in by ladies to the sound of a fanfare and the music of attendant minstrels. The peacock was reserved for the most elaborate feasts and was often served covered with gold leaf. At such feasts vows were sometimes sworn, the most famous occasion being the Feast of the Swans at Westminster in 1306 at which Edward I and his court vowed to avenge the murder of John Comyn, a pretender to the Scottish throne, by Robert Bruce. The particular representation in King's Lynn has been associated with a feast given to King Edward III there in 1344, but no documentary evidence for the link is known and it may instead portray an imaginary feast of birds described in a romance. Although the vessels on the table are not shown in any great detail, it is clear that they were intended to be depicted as more elaborate in form and number than those in the Luttrell psalter since there is a range of cups and standing vessels, some with handles and others with hexagonal bases.

In England the place of the host was often marked by the salt. The principal salt had a symbolic function, since it was brought in with some ceremony and set directly beside the host, thus marking the place of honour and the centre of the feast. An elaborate silver cup such as the fifteenth-century Lacock cup 48 may have fulfilled a similar function.

Before dining, the washing of hands was an important part of preparation for eating. It was the custom to wash the hands on entering the hall before meals. Many monasteries and large secular houses had wash basins and cisterns built in the passages leading to the refectory or hall. At Battle Hall in Kent, a washing place and cistern still exist. It is designed as a castle with two round battlemented towers, each with a spout in the form of a lion's head. Otherwise servants with a jug, bowl and towel would serve the diners. The water was sometimes warmed and scented with herbs, and

either the hands were washed in the basin or held out above it while water was poured over them from above. Gemellions, a pair of shallow 49 bowls, often enamelled, were used for this purpose in France in the thirteenth century. The side of one of the bowls had an outlet, often in the form of a lion's head, through which the water would be poured from the top to the bottom bowl. The interior of such bowls was frequently decorated with hunting scenes, combats, mythical animals or heraldry.

Sometimes bronze or pottery jugs were used as lavers (from the French *laver*, to wash). A bronze jug that was certainly used in this way 50 is the three-legged jug with a long spout ending in a dragon's head. Around the centre of this is the legend '*ie sui apelle lawr ie serf tut*

48 (*Opposite*) A secular silver cup of the fifteenth century, preserved as a chalice at the church of Lacock, Wiltshire.

49 (*Above*) A pair of French thirteenth-century enamelled gemellions decorated with heraldic shields.

50 (*Right*) Bronze laver or jug with animal spout. Fourteenth century.

51 Bronze aquamanile in the form of a knight on horseback. Late thirteenth century.

par amur' (I am called a laver, I serve all by love). Other tripod jugs of the fourteenth century bear the inscription *'venez laver'* (come to wash) around the middle and were presumably used with a large bronze bowl.

One of the most charming and elaborate of all water containers is the aquamanile – a vessel in the form of a lion, griffin or rider – which was used with a basin. At Durham, in the Benedictine monastery, every subprior had a 'ewer portrayed like unto an horse and a man sitting on his back as if he had been a-hunting, which served the subprior to wash'. The late thirteenth-century bronze aquamanile which was found in the River Tyne at Hexham illustrates this type of vessel. It is a finely modelled depiction of a knight sitting squarely on a surprisingly small horse. The vessel would have been filled through the hole in the top of the helmet and emptied through the spout in the nose of the horse.

Many of the books of courtesy and manners of the fifteenth century stress the need for washing the hands and cleanliness in general. For instance, William Caxton advises in his *Book of Curtesye*:

> Washe with water your hondes so cleene
> That in the towel shal no spotte be sene.

(Wash with water your hands so clean/that in the towel no spot shall be seen.)

In the fifteenth century the washing water was often kept in a niche in the wall where a spouted laver and towel were hung. Such lavers could be tipped so that the water poured out of one side. A laver dating from the second half of the fifteenth century swings from an upright handle held on either side of the rim by fixtures cast in the form of ladies' heads. It was emptied from the two spouts at each end, which ended in dragons' heads.

Careful washing of hands before and after meals was necessary because in the Middle

Ages people generally used only their fingers for eating. The custom of using a fork together with a knife to cut meat on a plate was a post-medieval invention, reputedly introduced into England from Italy by the eccentric traveller Thomas Coryat in the seventeenth century. Forks are mentioned in the thirteenth and fourteenth centuries, though they were evidently only intended for spearing sweet and sticky foods such as desserts, sweetmeats or fruit. A late fourteenth-century silver fork testifies to this, with its attached wire projection meant to prevent it falling into the serving dish.

Of the different kinds of cutlery, the knife was the most familiar and the most often used. Guests usually brought their own with them when they came to dine. The proper use of the knife was to cut meat from the bone into manageable pieces which could then be picked up by hand. It might also be used as a fork to spear a piece from a dish. Larger carving knives, often elaborately decorated, were necessary at every meal where joints and carcasses had to be dismembered. Carving was certainly not regarded as a menial task, since even great lords were honoured to carve at a royal feast. The importance of carving is matched by the elaborate decoration on the set of knives that belonged to the Duke of Burgundy (see p.19). The set contains two types of knives – two small ones with sharp points and two larger ones with broad thin blades, used for offering a slice of meat to the Duke. The wooden handles of the knives are inlaid with silver enamelled with the arms of the Dukes of Burgundy and the motto '*s'il plaist a dieu*' (if it pleases God). The words are divided and surrounded by foliage.

Spoons used every day were made of simple materials such as wood, metal or horn. Of these, horn was the favourite. Silver spoons were treasured and were passed down from generation to generation in wills. The bowl of the medieval spoon was pear-shaped, tapering to the stem. Sometimes the handle ended in an ornamental top, shaped as an acorn or a diamond point. In the fifteenth century the head of the Virgin first appears in this position, and spoons so decorated are known as maiden

54 A Flemish fifteenth-century silver gilt spoon decorated with enamelled flowers and the inscription 'ave maria'.

head spoons. A rare example of a richly decorated spoon is the silver gilt Flemish travelling spoon, the bowl of which is en- ₅₄ amelled on both sides with leaves and flowers in green and red enamel with the legend 'ave maria' (Hail Mary) in the centre of the bowl. The bowl is joined to the stem by the head of a monster and the hexagonal stem, decorated with enamel, ends in a strawberry knop.

Nuts were eaten at the end of the meal as well as being used in cooking. The elaborate decoration of the bronze nut crackers suggests ₅₅ that this example was used at the table rather than in the kitchen. The handles, ending in human heads, are decorated with a bird and hound, and the nippers are engraved with lions' heads.

Illustrations of feasting show kings, nobles, gentlemen and rich merchants, among whom polite customs and conventions – and therefore more highly decorated objects such as knives and spoons – were more likely to be common. We know far less about the ways of the poorer classes, although recent archaeological and historical work has provided more evidence of the range of materials and vessels used for preparing food and cooking in the medieval period. Pottery was the cheapest and most widespread. Metal vessels, especially of bronze, were increasingly used in the later Middle Ages, and in this period some of the pottery vessels imitate metal shapes. Inventories suggest that by the end of the thirteenth century metal vessels for cooking were widespread among the traders, merchants and craftsmen of a provincial town. The list of objects valued at Colchester in Essex for the subsidy of 1301 indicates that a large proportion of the wealthier inhabitants possessed a bronze ewer and basin for hand-washing, and perhaps also a cup of silver or of decorated wood (mazer) (see p.47) and a couple of silver spoons as well as the essential range of bronze cooking pots and pans.

It is very unusual for cooking vessels to be decorated. Even in the scene of John of Gaunt feasting there is no sign of decoration on the cooking vessels. However, possibly because they had a longer life, the stone or metal mortars used for grinding herbs and spices were sometimes adorned with human faces at the corners.

Roasting and stewing were common methods of cooking. For stewing, pots were suspended over the fire, pushed into the embers or placed on a trivet. Both pottery vessels and metal cauldrons were used. The cauldron was generally of cast bronze standing on three legs and lifted by two lug handles springing from the top rim. An engraving published in 1801 records a particularly fine example of a metal cauldron which has since disappeared. It is unusual in being covered with decoration. There are two bands of inscription, the symbols of the four evangelists above the upper line of inscription and mythical animals such as the griffin and unicorn between the two lines, as well as fleurs-de-lis and four-petalled rosettes scattered over the upper surface of the pot. The lower inscription reads '*vilelinus angetel me fecit fieri*' (William Angetel had me made), indicating the proud owner of the pot. The upper inscription in smaller characters reads:

ie su pot de graunt honhur
viaunde a fere de bon savhur.

(I am a pot of great honour/To give the meat such good flavour.)

The cauldron was primarily used for stewing meat. Other smaller vessels, equivalent to modern saucepans, were called skillets, posnets or pipkins, and these were cast bronze miniature cauldrons with a handle attached to the rim. The legs would be used to set the vessel above the embers of the fire. A posnet was bought for the Lady Elizabeth, daughter of Edward I, when she was at Rhuddlan Castle in North Wales in the winter of 1281. These smaller vessels, used for sauces and cooking vegetables, increased in popularity and were common in the post-medieval period.

Among the vessels used on the table there was a distinct hierarchy of materials. Gold, silver and silver gilt were the most prized, and vessels of less expensive materials were often mounted with them. Silver spoons were the most common pieces of silver. Owing to their value as precious metal, only a few silver bowls and dishes have survived.

55 A pair of fifteenth-century bronze nut crackers.

56 Engraving of a fourteenth-century cooking pot, now lost, which has an inscription indicating that it was made for William Angetel.

The small hexagonal silver jug represents a ₅₉ type of vessel that was common in the four-teenth century and can be seen in paintings of feasts. The simplicity of the sides is con-tinued upwards to the lid and knop and is also reflected in the simple square-sectioned handle. Apart from the shape, the only decora-tion is the lines of beading around the base, lid and top of the vessel. The spout ends in a dragon's head.

Silver bowls and dishes were often dec-orated with arms and inscriptions, but few of these have survived. The silver bowl in the Victoria and Albert Museum, known as the ₅₈ Studley bowl from its association with the church of Studley near Fountains Abbey in Yorkshire, is gilt on the outside of the cover and bowl, except for the inscription. The outside of both cover and bowl are engraved

57 Silver gilt drinking cup with a curved handle. French or German, fifteenth century.

44

with a black letter inscription amidst foliage which begins with a cross followed by the alphabet. A similar vessel, a silver bowl with an alphabet on the cover, was bequeathed by John Morton of York in 1431; such a vessel may well have been made for a rich or noble child.

The fourteenth and fifteenth centuries show an increase in the popularity of pewter in contrast to articles made of cheaper materials such as wood, clay, stone and leather. While the cellarer of Battle Abbey, in Sussex, thought clay or wooden dishes were suitable purchases for the visit of Edward I in the winter of 1275, almost a hundred years later in 1359–60 pewter dishes, plates and cruets were being purchased for the use of the monks. Pewter kitchenware and tableware were popular since they could give the impression that they were made of silver and were less likely to be broken in transport than either clay or wood.

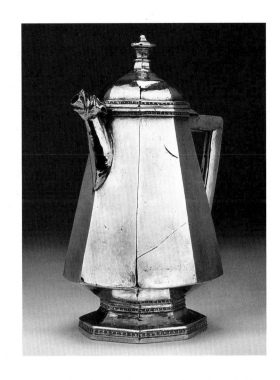

59 (*Above*) Late fourteenth-century silver jug, probably made in Burgundy.

58 (*Left*) Silver gilt bowl and cover engraved with a black letter alphabet. Made *c.*1400, it is known as the Studley bowl, from its association with Studley church, near Ripon.

Wooden vessels were far more widespread than their survival today would indicate. Excavations in medieval towns such as Perth in Scotland and Southampton have produced examples of plain wooden vessels. There are two types, either turned on a lathe or made up of sections of staves. Lathe-turned vessels were often produced from spotted wood. Their name of mazers is derived from the Old High German *másá*, a spot, and they were often made from the spotted or speckled variety of wood known as bird's-eye maple. As prized objects they were often mounted in silver. This mazer has silver-gilt mounts on the foot and top of the lid. The foot has lozenge-shaped enamels with, against a blue ground, a silver bird with green wings that has a shield hanging from its neck bearing the arms of Flanders. The same bird in the same colours appears on the lid of the mazer. From these arms it has been suggested that the mazer may have belonged to Louis of Flanders, illegitimate son of Louis de Mâle, who was Count of Flanders from 1346 to 1384.

The range of materials from silver to pottery and their decoration reflect the sense of hierarchy present in the formal proceedings of medieval feasting. However, the decoration of the jugs on the medieval table shows much greater life and vivacity.

Most pieces were undecorated and it is only on the more elaborate and expensive ones that decorations or inscriptions occur. The main themes for jugs and bowls used on the table were animals and human faces. Animals were most commonly used for the decoration of spouts, as can be seen on the laver, or the silver cruet. Dragon-like animals occur in the diamond-shaped lozenges of the jug found in Cannon Street, London.

The making of bronze and pottery vessels in the shape of animals or mounted knights is a characteristic of the Middle Ages. We have seen (p.40) that the aquamanile from the

61 Pottery jug decorated with dragons in lozenges. Found in London. English, late thirteenth century.

60 Late fourteenth-century wooden mazer mounted with a silver knop and foot. On the foot and on the shield, hanging from the bird's neck, are the arms of Flanders.

River Tyne was made in the form of a mounted knight. Pottery jugs in the shape of people give a most lively effect. The small green-glazed jug 62 is modelled in the form of a man with round eyes and outstanding ears, and with two hands pulling at his beard. A stately woman inside front cover forms the green-glazed jug from Worcester. Her face, with eyes, nose, mouth and dimpled chin, is on the front while her hair is bunched up at the back. Her neck and body form the neck and body of the jug. The lady holding a fish against her cheek and bare breast, also 64 from Worcester, may have formed part of a statuette that stood on the table or perhaps was part of a salt.

Decoration with faces is common on medieval sculpture, particularly the gargoyles and capitals of medieval churches. This may have inspired the use of the human face as decoration on jugs, where it sometimes occurs on the side of the rim, decorating the spout, or on the body of the vessel. Faces are even found on the top or bottom of handles. An unusual use of the face is to be seen on the top of a bronze jug. Here the face is fully modelled 63 with knitted brows, half-round eyes and thick lips above the pointed beard which forms the cover of the spout.

Occasionally scenes of action with human figures occur, such as the hunting scene on the jug from Earlswood in Surrey. The decoration, 65 modelled in white slip in a form of white silhouette, shows a huntsman blowing his horn with his dogs in pursuit of a stag.

A fuller form of modelling is found on the Knight jug from the Moot Hall, Nottingham. 66 This fine jug, made at the kilns in Scarborough (Yorkshire) in the thirteenth century, is the most remarkable example known of modelling on English medieval pottery. The decoration on the upper part of the jug shows four knights with shields on horseback, while beneath them is a stag hunt with three stags being chased and attacked by four hounds. The

62 A small green-glazed pottery jug in human form. The arms are indicated by applied pieces of clay and the beard and hands by incised lines. *c.* 1300.

63 (*Right*) The face on the lid of a bronze jug. English, fourteenth century.

64 (*Right*) Pottery fragment in the form of a lady with a fish. Found at Worcester. Fourteenth century.

65 (*Left*) Early thirteenth-century pottery jug showing hunting scenes. Found at Earlswood, Surrey.

66 (*Right*) Thirteenth-century pottery jug decorated with modelled knights. Found at the Moot Hall, Nottingham, but made at Scarborough, *c.*1300.

twisted handle and spout in the form of a man balances the decoration on the top.

The Nottingham jug is only one of a whole group of such vessels produced at kiln sites in England ranging from Scarborough, Grimston and Lincoln to Bristol. The products from the kilns in the east of England were widely exported across the North Sea and would have graced tables in Bergen and Borgund in Scandinavia and Bruges and Aardenburg in Flanders.

67 Another example of human decoration occurs on the Exeter jug, discovered in South Street, Exeter, in 1899. This is an exceptional piece of the type of polychrome pottery produced in south-west France around 1300. The pot is in the form of a three-storeyed house or castle. The top storey is decorated with five conventional shields. Inside the house are two figures of bishops. From the windows of the first storey lean figures of women listening to minstrels beneath playing stringed instruments. The exact meaning of the decoration is not clear but it is probably meant to be a satirical comment on the behaviour of bishops associating with young women in houses of ill repute. This remarkable vessel is probably the earliest known medieval puzzle jug. In this vessel the liquid runs down the hollow handle into the base of the jug and is emptied through the neck and the head of the long-eared animal, possibly a horse or a mule, on the other side. It is a *tour de force* by a potter with considerable ability in construction of vessels, the modelling of figures and the painting and glazing of the surface of such pots. A puzzle jug would have been brought out either between courses or at the end of the meal to amuse the company.

Heraldic shields were sometimes used as a decorative feature on vessels. The shields around the top of the Exeter puzzle jug have no specific heraldic meaning but are purely decorative. However, as we have seen (p.47), the bird with the shield of Flanders on the top of the mazer served as an indication of the family 60 of the owner.

Inscriptions, more common on bronze than pottery vessels, were often used for decorative effect to provide a horizontal band of lettering. Sometimes the inscription indicates the function of the vessel, as we have already seen on the bronze laver, where the inscription de- 50 clares '*ie sui appelle lawr ie serf tut par amur*' (I am called a laver, I serve all by love). The inscription on the hunting pot (p.44) not only 56 relates to its use but also indicates the person for whom it was made. The personal possession of pots was the main reason for their inscription, and some utter threats against potential thieves. A bronze jug found in Gower in Wales bears the words '*ie sui lawr gilebert ki memblera mal i dedert*' (I am the laver of Gilbert, evil will come to whoever carries me off).

Other inscriptions on pots relate to graces to be said before meals. The Danish horn with bird-like claw supports has a copper-gilt 68 mount around the mouth with the inscription '*potum deus benedicat*' (God blesses the drink). Sometimes lettering may be used for its decorative effect, as on the Studley bowl (see 58 p.44), but occasionally it was simply used for the proverbial wisdom of the fireplace. One bronze jug bears the words '*sai wel or pes*' (Speak well or keep quiet), while the longest inscriptions known occur on two late fourteenth-century jugs bearing the royal arms. One, in the Victoria and Albert Museum, is decorated with:

> Goddis Grace be in this place. Amen.
> Stond uttir from the fyre
> And lat on lust come nere.

(The Grace of God be in this place. Amen./Stand away from the fire/And let who wishes come near.)

The Ashanti ewer bears an impressive array 69 of heraldry, badges and inscriptions. This

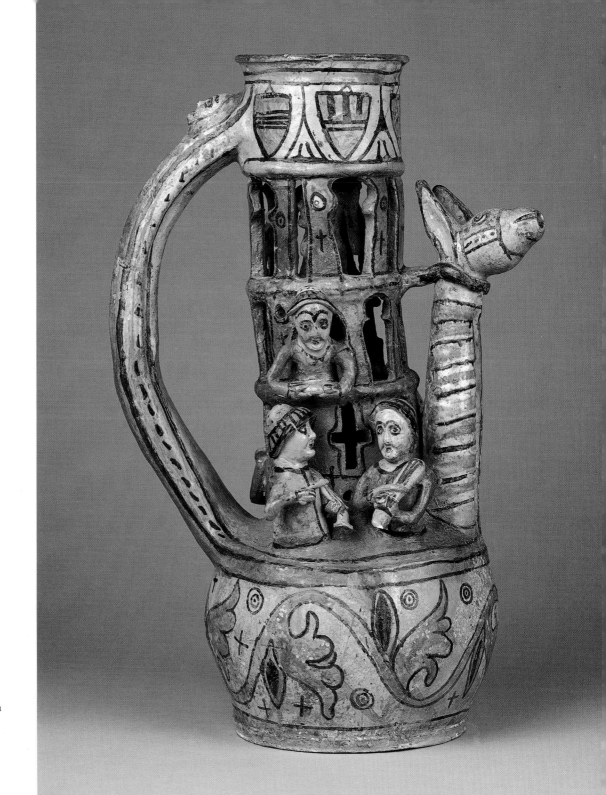

67 Pottery puzzle jug made in the Saintonge in south-west France and found in Exeter. French, *c.*1300.

68 Fifteenth-century Danish drinking horn mounted in silver gilt with claws.

69 Bronze jug with the arms and royal badges of King Richard II of England. Decorated with three bands of inscriptions. Found in the Royal Palace of the Ashanti at Kumasi in 1896.

remarkable bronze vessel was found in the temple of the kings of Ashanti at Kumasi in Africa in 1896, although how it came to be there is a complete mystery. It bears on the front the royal arms of the kings of England from 1340 to 1405 (see p.29), but can be dated more precisely to the reign of Richard II (1377–99) by the badges on the lid. These show the lion, a royal badge, and the white hart which was Richard's personal badge (see p.33). The exterior of the base of the jug is decorated with two proverbs, arranged in three lines and reading from the bottom upwards. The proverbs may be divided into four lines:

> He that wyl not spare when he may
> He shal not spend when he would.
> Deme the best in every dowt
> Til the trowthe be truid owte.

(He who will not save when he can/will not be able to spend when he wants to./Hope for the best whenever there is doubt,/until the truth is established.)

The proverbial comments on jugs may echo the wisdom of the fool. Entertainment provided by both fools and minstrels was a characteristic part of the feast. The importance 47 of music can be seen in the Peacock Feast (see p.37). Fools also provided diversion. When in captivity in England, John II, King of France (1350–64), brought his own fool with him who took his meals at the same time as the King and was treated in a privileged manner. Fools often carried a bauble as a mark of their profession and this wand of office often ended 70 in a fool's head. Laughter, wit and music created an atmosphere of celebration and a strong sense of occasion at feasts, and this is reflected in the decoration of the most elaborate ceremonial utensils.

70 Fifteenth-century bronze head of a fool from a jester's bauble.

4 Romance and courtly love

Romance and courtly love provided a rich source for both poetry and the decorative arts in the medieval period. Romances are essentially stories of heroes or lovers derived from the French word *roman*. Such stories could include tales of courtly love among other tales of heroic exploits.

The new concept of courtly love, first expressed in troubadour poetry, appeared at the end of the eleventh century in Languedoc in the south of France. A highly formalised mode of behaviour, it combines the concepts of humility, courtesy and devotion to the ideal of love. The lover serves his lady in a manner closely modelled on the service a feudal vassal owed to his lord. This attitude to love developed in castles and courts where, in an atmosphere of leisure and luxury, there were many young men but comparatively few women. The lady of the castle and her damsels set the ideal of manners and social behaviour. The arrangement of marriages for reasons of politics or to increase landed territory was common. As a reaction, love was treated as an end in itself, often leading to a neglect of the marriage vows.

The classical Latin poet Ovid enjoyed great popularity in the medieval period. His most delightful and sophisticated work was the *Ars Amatoria* (Art of Love) which explains the technique of finding, winning and enjoying a lover: in the Middle Ages he was known by the title 'Teacher of Love.' Classical influence in the Middle Ages is shown by the classical intaglio showing Venus which was set in silver 71 in the thirteenth century for use as a seal matrix. Around the intaglio was engraved the legend '*ie sui sel de amur lel*' (I am a seal of loyal love), showing how classical objects were used by medieval lovers.

Episodes of courtly love are illustrated in the scenes on the late twelfth-century casket belonging to the enamellers' tradition of Limoges 72 in south-west France. The casket has been ascribed to the court of Aquitaine. Eleanor of Aquitaine, the wife of Henry II of England, and her sons and daughters seem to have played an important role in the diffusion and development of romances.

The top and sides of the casket depict scenes in the life of the knight both in the hall and at war: warriors are shown in combat and minstrels serenade their lady, a warrior fights a lion, and there are grotesque animals and dancers. On the top and front are scenes of lovers. On the left of the casket a minstrel front cover playing a stringed instrument with a bow serenades a dancing lady. A bird, perhaps symbolising love, flies between them. On the right a lover is about to kneel before his lady, who holds him with a halter around the neck with one hand while with her other she grasps a bird.

Between the two couples is a mysterious figure in black with a horn around his neck, who holds a raised sword in his right hand

71 Venus holds a bearded mask in front of a statue of a youth on this classical intaglio set in a thirteenth-century silver seal.

towards the dancing couple on the left, and a key in his left hand towards the lover and his lady on the right. The exact meaning of this figure is not clear, but perhaps he is meant to underline the contrast between the strength of the man (symbolised by the sword) and the strength of the lady and her love (symbolised by the key).

The figure of the lover before his lady on the right-hand side of the casket clearly shows how the service of the lover to his lady was modelled on that of a feudal vassal to his lord, since in the feudal gesture of receiving lordship the vassal knelt and placed his hands together in those of the lord. The casket is a remarkable evocation of the attributes of grace and courage, and of the sadness and joy celebrated in the troubadour poetry of the court of Aquitaine.

The range of subjects in romances was a fruitful source for the decoration of medieval objects. One of the most popular stories of the Middle Ages was that of Tristram and Isolde, widely used as a source for the decoration of manuscripts, embroideries, ivory caskets, wall paintings and tiles. The best-known English poem retelling the story, probably from a French source, was written by the poet Thomas in the twelfth century.

A fine narrative series of scenes from the romance of Tristram occurs on the remarkable late thirteenth-century tiles from Chertsey 73, 7 Abbey. Discovered during building work in the 1850s, the tiles are very fragmentary although some have been restored in modern times. The version of the story they follow is that of Thomas, but in so far as they survive they place greater emphasis on the early part of the story which relates to the heroic achievements and battles of Tristram rather than his love of Isolde.

The series of drawings and the plate show six of the scenes. Tristram, a skilful hunter and harpist, impresses King Mark of Cornwall. Mark, wearing a crown, reclines on a couch while Tristram, a simple band round his head, plays the harp. On learning that the King of Ireland exacts a tribute of the sons of Cornish nobles, and seeing the barons lamenting for their sons, Tristram offers himself as the champion of Cornwall to meet Morhaut, the Irish ambassador, in single combat, staking the tribute on the outcome of the fight. When Mark learns of Tristram's intention, he kisses him. Tristram kills Morhaut but is poisoned by a wound. Mark visits Tristram on his sick bed.

The Queen of Ireland nurses Tristram, and when his wound is healed the hero undertakes to teach her daughter Isolde to play the harp. On his return to Cornwall he praises Isolde.

73 Drawings of late thirteenth-century tiles from Chertsey Abbey showing scenes from the story of Tristram and Isolde. (*Top left*) Tristram plays the harp before King Mark. (*Top right*) The Cornish barons lament for their sons, who are seated at their feet. (*Bottom left*) Mark visits the sick Tristram. (*Bottom right*) Tristram teaches Isolde to play the harp.

74 Isolde, in a becalmed boat, attempts to reach Tristram, as depicted on a late thirteenth-century tile from Chertsey Abbey.

75 Lid of a bone casket, carved in Cologne in the early thirteenth century, showing Brangwain bringing Tristram and Isolde the love potion.

King Mark decides to send Tristram back to Ireland to ask for the hand of Isolde in marriage for himself. Tristram returns to Ireland and, having performed valuable service to the King of Ireland, asks as a reward the hand of Isolde for Mark. Isolde and Brangwain, her attendant, set off for Cornwall with Tristram. Brangwain has received from Isolde's mother a love potion to be given to Mark. On the ship Tristram and Isolde find the potion, drink it and are forever in love. Mark and Isolde are married, but the relations between Tristram and Isolde continue and the lovers are eventually betrayed to Mark. Tristram is banished and, when dying in Brittany, sends for Isolde. If she comes, the ship is to bear a white sail, if not, a black. A jealous rival also called Isolde (of Brittany) overhears this and, when the ship returns, tells Tristram that the sail is black. Tristram despairs and dies. The last scene illustrated here from the Chertsey tiles shows a ship becalmed off the coast of Brittany. Isolde, in front of the mast, is greatly tormented and gesticulates to the oarsman in the bow, ordering him to row to the coast. All is in vain, however, since Isolde finds Tristram

75

74

dead and, herself despairing, dies beside him.

The nature of the story indicates that the tiles were unlikely to have been specifically designed and made for the rich Benedictine abbey of Chertsey but were more probably ordered and made for one of the royal palaces of Henry III, such as Westminster or Winchester. We know that Henry III, who possessed a great book of romances, was particularly fond of them as subjects for wall paintings and he commissioned the romance of Alexander to be painted on the walls of Nottingham Castle and Clarendon Palace.

One of the earliest representations of the romance of Tristram and Isolde is on the lid of a bone casket, carved in Cologne in the early thirteenth century. It centres on the turning point of the story, depicting Brangwain bringing to the hero and heroine the potion that was to have such a devastating effect.

Lancelot was the great hero of the Arthurian cycle. Despite his fame as a lover of Guinevere, the Queen of King Arthur, in the romances he only rarely makes an appearance (except in illuminated manuscripts) on objects of medieval art. He is depicted on a group of early fourteenth-century ivory caskets made in Paris, on which he is shown attempting to reach the castle where the Queen is imprisoned. This episode involves the hero crossing a black raging stream spanned only by a sword. The sword is as long as two lances and each end is fixed in a tree-trunk. This particular scene is depicted on the back of the ivory casket. Although there are three other scenes on the back, the four scenes do not form a narrative sequence telling the whole of Lancelot's story, and the continuation of the row of spears over the two central scenes suggests that the ivory carver had little first-hand knowledge of the literary sources.

Not all romances derived from legendary sources: some told contemporary stories of love. One that attracted the attention of ivory carvers in Paris during the fourteenth century, which therefore occurs on several ivory caskets, concerns the Châtelaine (Lady) de Vergi. In this story the Châtelaine, a niece of the Duke

76 Back panel of a French fourteenth-century ivory casket showing Lancelot attacking the phantom lion and crossing the sword bridge threatened by spears from above.

of Burgundy, was loved by a knight in the Duke's court. To keep their meetings secret she had trained her pet dog to go out to signal that she was free to meet her lover. Meanwhile the Duke's wife, the Duchess, made advances to the knight and, on his rejection of her, accused him to the Duke. The Duke condemned the knight to exile, but rather than be separated from his love he told his secret. The Duke went to the garden and saw the dog and the meeting of the lovers. Although he had agreed to keep their secret, he confided in the Duchess, adding that she would die if she revealed it.

At a court dance, however, the Duchess taunted the Lady about her dog. The Lady, thinking her knight had betrayed her, went to her room and died of sorrow on her bed. The knight went to her, found her dead and committed suicide. The Duke followed, found the bodies, drew the sword from the body of

the knight and killed the Duchess with it. The bodies of the lovers were buried in one grave and the Duke joined a Crusade from which he never returned.

This story was written in the second half of the thirteenth century. The caskets that illustrate it depict the whole tale in narrative scenes. The lid of the casket in the British Museum shows the beginning of the story in a series of barbed quatrefoils. On the left half of the lid, in the two upper compartments, the Lady meets her lover and explains her plan of employing the dog. Underneath she sends the dog and meets her lover. On the right half of the lid the Duchess tempts the knight, and then tells the Duke. The Duke draws his sword on the knight, but is reconciled upon hearing his explanation. The rest of the story is told around the back, sides and front of the casket, culminating in the death of the Duchess.

77

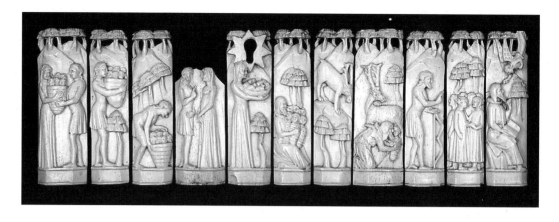

78 Fragments of an early fifteenth-century Italian bone casket illustrating part of the romance of the Knight of the Swan.

Fragments of an Italian casket of the fifteenth century illustrate a part of the romance of the Knight of the Swan, also known as the story of Mattabruna, and perhaps best known today as the preface to the story of Lohengrin. Mattabruna is the wicked stepmother of a queen. She substitutes a litter of puppies for the newly born children of her stepdaughter and gives the children to a servant to be killed. He takes pity on the children, however, and leaves them near the cell of a hermit who brings them up.

After several years, Rudemard, Mattabruna's steward, sees the children with gold chains around their necks. Mattabruna orders him to cut off the chains and he obtains all but one, which belongs to a girl. When the chains are removed, the children are changed into swans and fly to a lake near the palace. After a long period their sister, whose chain has not been removed and who therefore keeps her human form, comes to the palace, recognises Rudemard and tells her father the King the truth. The King orders the chains to be restored and the swans assume human form, except for one brother whose chain has already been melted down: he has to remain a swan. Helias, the most valiant of the brothers, insists on the restoration of his mother to the King's favour. Rudemard is then killed, Matta-

bruna burnt and Helias sets forth on his adventures in a boat drawn by his swan brother. He thus becomes known as the Knight of the Swan.

The casket fragments show the earlier part of the story. They depict Mattabruna delivering the infants to a servant to hide in the wood, the substitution of the puppies, and the bringing up of the children at the hermitage. The last fragments may represent Rudemard and the children before the removal of their gold chains caused them to change into swans. The long thin shape of the panels is determined by the bone from which they were carved.

Some aristocratic families traced their descent, most usually through the Counts of Boulogne, from the Knight of the Swan who featured in this legend. Such families often used the badge of the swan as their distinguishing mark. The Dunstable Swan Jewel (see p.33) is one of the best examples of this tradition. The gold chain attached to the coronet around the swan's neck reflects the story.

Not all the decoration on secular ivory caskets was in the form of a narrative illustrating romances. There were illustrations of a variety of scenes of lovers or scenes drawn from romance, allegory or satire. Some of these caskets portray, on the lid, the Assault

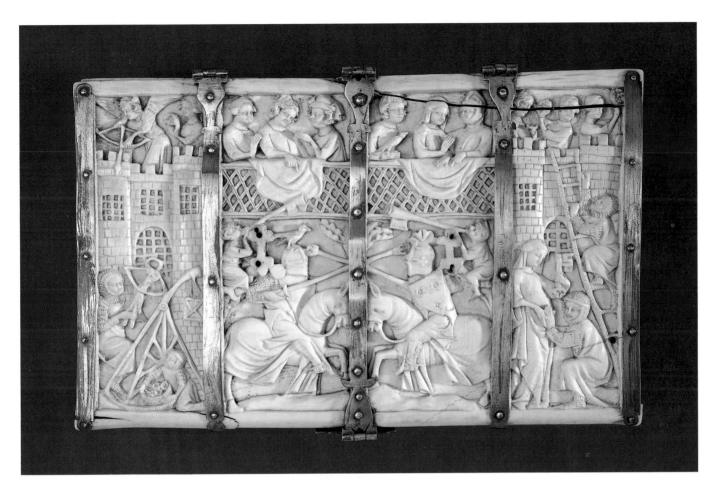

79 Lid of a French fourteenth-century ivory casket showing the Assault on the Castle of Love.

on the Castle of Love. The lid illustrated shows in the centre mounted knights jousting while heralds blow trumpets from their seats in the trees above. One of the knights bears on his shield a device of three roses. Their ladies look on from the balconies above. To the left the winged God of Love aims an arrow down on the besiegers who are preparing to attack the castle with a crossbow and a trebuchet (usually used for launching stones) loaded with roses. On the right a knight kneels before his lady to receive the key of the castle; another knight scales the walls on a ladder while the ladies above hurl down baskets of roses.

No literary source for this scene of the Assault on the Castle of Love has ever been satisfactorily established. The only surviving illustration of the scene earlier in date than the ivories is in the Peterborough psalter, a late thirteenth-century English manuscript, now in Brussels. Here one of the knights again bears on his shield the device of three roses, while the lady defenders carry standards with four roses. The defenders seem to be getting the upper hand over the knights. The illumination bears out the evidence of documentary references to festivals in which such assaults occurred. It is clear that the theme was current well before the ivories were carved. The visual metaphor depends on the idea of the defence of feminine chastity, shown as the defence of a tower or castle.

The caskets with the Castle of Love on the lid have a variety of scenes on the sides. The British Museum example bears scenes from the Tristram and Lancelot romances as well as the legends of the Fountain of Youth and the Capture of the Unicorn. Others depict scenes of lovers meeting, gifts exchanged between lovers, and lovers playing chess. Such scenes also occur singly on mirror cases or writing tablets. The pair of tablets illustrated show a lady and a knight conversing as they ride out hawking, and a kneeling knight presenting a rose for a wreath that a lady stands holding in her left hand. The inside of these writing tablets would have been coated with a mixture of wax and pitch or resin so that they were usually black. This surface was then written on with a metal-tipped stylus of bone. By smoothing the wax the writer could erase or correct what he had written. Since these tablets are so often decorated with romantic scenes, it is tempting to suppose that they were sometimes used for written campaigns of love.

Another ivory writing tablet is of particular interest since it shows a party game in progress. This is the game of hot cockles, perhaps played after feasts. A blindfolded man kneels with his head in a lady's lap. He has to guess which of the ladies with hands raised is striking him. As soon as his guess is correct,

80 (*Below*) Pair of French fourteenth-century writing tablets, showing a hawking scene on one side and on the other a knight presenting a rose to a lady.

81 (*Below right*) A French fourteenth-century writing tablet showing a game of forfeits.

the bearded man kneeling behind him will take his place, while the pair kissing behind the lady no doubt represent the successful conclusion of a previous game.

Love scenes occasionally occur on other objects. A remarkable and unusual upper part of a shoe, found in London in the mid nineteenth century, has delicate cut-out and incised decoration and inscriptions. In the centre roundel on one side an elderly man offers a circular object, perhaps a coin, to a young woman whose long hair suggests that she is of easy virtue. The scene may well be an example of the motif of the unequal lovers, lovers unmatched in size or age. On one side of the main roundel a young man holds out a mirror to a monkey and on the other a young girl is beating a dog. The shoe seems to represent a comment on the follies of love, such as vanity or cruelty.

82 (*Above*) Drawing of a late fourteenth-century leather shoe found in London.

83 (*Right*) Two scenes of lovers on the 'Talbot' casket, made in northern France or Flanders in the late fourteenth century.

84 (*Right*) Gold ring engraved on the outside with a grammatical inscription, and on the inside with a figure of a lady with a squirrel. French, late fourteenth century.

Wooden caskets covered with leather were popular in the late fourteenth and fifteenth centuries; for whatever reason, perhaps because ivory became scarce, the Parisian ivory caskets enjoyed only a brief and limited period of popularity during the fourteenth century. Sometimes the leather caskets have lovers depicted on them. The so-called 'Talbot casket', made in northern France or Flanders in the late fourteenth century, is decorated in raised and moulded leather with a series of scenes of lovers. One side shows a dejected falconer with his hand in a bag feeding his bird while his lady stands opposite. The accompanying panel portrays a pair of lovers embracing and kissing each other. The two panels contrast the state of the dejected and the happy lover.

As well as the romance scenes examined above, symbols were often used to express love. The sport of hawking and falconry lent itself to this symbolic treatment and was frequently employed as a motif on seals and ivories. One of the most common types of seal used for letters shows a hawk preying on another bird with the inscription '*alas ie su pris*' (alas, I am caught), presumably a reference to a lover's capitulation.

A symbolic meaning was often bestowed upon animals. The squirrel, sometimes tamed to serve as a lady's pet, may be seen held on the arm of the Queen, possibly Eleanor of Castile, the wife of Edward I, who is depicted on the Chertsey tiles. This animal is also occasionally depicted in association with inscriptions concerning love. The gold ring set with a sapphire bears an elaborate inscription (see p.69) and, inside, a lady holding a squirrel on a leash.

A group of seal dies has figures of squirrels in the centre with the inscription 'I crack nuts', and the squirrel cracking a nut was one of the objects produced from the mould. The allusion may simply be to the similarity between the cracking of a nutshell to obtain the sweet

kernel of the nut and the breaking of a seal to obtain a sweet message, but in thirteenth-century France the cracking of nuts by a squirrel was certainly used as sexual innuendo. In *L'Esquiriel*, a story dating from the same period, Robin's squirrel searches in the 'belly' of the heroine for nuts eaten the day before; elsewhere, in response to her interest in the commotion under his clothes, he explains that the squirrel is coming up out of its hole.

The ram was used in the Middle Ages as a symbol of lust and this may explain a scene on the back of the Warwick gittern. Here, above a mask, two rams reach up to eat the foliage of a tree while the figure beneath is making a very distinctive gesture. He is girning – pulling down an eye to make a deliberately distorted face – in a gesture known as the eyelid pull, meaning 'you can't fool me'.

In contrast, the gesture of clasping hands represented, as it still does, fidelity and love. It appears on the brooches that were made from the bronze mould (see p.15): this has clasped

contents page

85 (*Right*) Impression of the seal of Christian Sprotforth on which flowers sprout forth from a heart. English, fourteenth century.

86 (*Below*) Gold brooch with an inscription of love engraved between red rubies and blue sapphires. Thirteenth century.

hands at the side while the pin is formed by an arrow piercing a heart. The clasping of hands was part of the betrothal ritual, and rings decorated with clasped hands often have love inscriptions on them. A gold stirrup-shaped ring set with a sapphire found in Hatfield Forest, Essex, combines the motif with the inscription '*ie sui de druerie, si ne me donei mie*' (I am a love token, do not give me away). It is impossible to decide today whether such rings commemorate friendship, love, betrothal or marriage; in fact, the same ring may have served all these purposes.

Opposed heads – the head of a man facing that of a woman – are another symbol of love. A good example is the seal of Christian Sprot- 85 forth, who chose as his device a lily with three flowers issuing from a heart placed between the faces of a man and woman, thus indicating, by a rebus or pun on the owner's name, how love sprouted forth from the heart.

Another symbol of love, which occurs in many forms and which is still used, was the heart. This appears as the shape for a pendant or brooch or even a book; in the motif of the flowering heart; or as a symbol in inscriptions. Heart-shaped brooches were exchanged between lovers, such gifts enabling them to indicate that they had given their heart (either love or brooch) to their lover. The fifteenth-century French poet Charles of Orleans advises the courtier how he could combine the gift of a replica of his heart with the traditional gift of the lover – the expensive present:

Some thing devise, and take [it] for thyn ese,
And send it to her, that may her herte apese:
Some hert, or ring, or lettre, or device,
Or precious stone; but spare not for no price.

(Think of something which may soften her heart, and send it to her to ease your pain [of love]: some heart, or ring, or letter, or device, or precious stone; but do not spare the cost.)

Just such an expensive present could have
86 been the gold lover's brooch, set alternately
with red rubies and blue sapphires between
which is engraved the inscription '*io sui ici
en liu dami amo*' (I am here in place of a
lover, love), or again the heart-shaped brooch
87 around which is entwined a scroll bearing the
words '*vous estes ma ioy moundeine*' (You are
my earthly love).

One of the most delightful examples of the
88 heart shape occurs with the pendant found at
Rocklea Sands near Poole in Dorset. One side
of the heart-shaped pendant, which is suspended from a chain, is filled with tears. These
would have originally stood out against a
background of enamel or niello, none of which
now remains. On the other side is a five-
petalled leaf, perhaps an ivy leaf, and the
black-letter inscription '*tristes en plesire*' (sadness in pleasure), which echoes the device of
the tears contained in the heart.

87 (*Right*) Gold heart-shaped
brooch with entwined scroll.
Fifteenth century.

88 (*Left above and below*) Gold heart-shaped pendant found at Rocklea Sands. French, fifteenth century.

Tears occur occasionally on fifteenth-century jewellery, often in combination with an inscription. A reference to a pendant decorated with tears which is remarkably close to the Poole pendant appears in the *Arrêts d'Amour*, a series of mock lawsuits written by Martial d'Auvergne around 1460. In one of these a lover, complaining that his lady has forsaken him, proves her previous attachment by producing her gift of 'a little gold heart decorated with tears, which he had always worn, and still wore, for her love between his flesh and his shirt'.

The concept of tears within the heart lies behind one of the verses in a poem by Charles d'Orleans:

> *Dedens mon Livre de Pensée*
> *J'ay trouvé escripvant mon cueur*
> *La vray histoire de douleur*
> *De larmes toutes enluminée.*

(In the book of my thoughts/I have found written on my heart/The true history of sorrow/Decorated with tears.)

89 (*Right*) Gold inscribed brooch found at Writtle, Essex. Thirteenth century.

The flowering heart demonstrated the growth of love from the heart. It is most clearly expressed on a seal where two hands support a heart amidst floral scrolls with the legend '*ieo tene le qor ma mie*' (I hold thy heart my love.) The motif was used in both secular and religious contexts and occurs on silver rings and on tiles.

The widespread use of inscriptions is one of the characteristic features of medieval rings and brooches. The heart also appears as a motif in inscriptions. For instance, instead of the inscription '*mon cuer avez*', '*mon ♥ avez*' was sometimes used. Inscriptions on rings and brooches in the Middle Ages often repeat each other to the point of banality. The most common is undoubtedly '*amor vincit omnia*' (Love conquers all); '*mon cuer avez*' (You have my heart) is also very frequent. This makes the longer and more complicated inscriptions all the more interesting. On the gold brooch from 89 Writtle, in Essex, is engraved:

> *ieo sui fermail pur garder sein*
> *ke nu svilein nimette mein*

(I am a brooch to guard the breast/so that no rascal may put his hand thereon.)

The ring showing the lady with the squirrel 84 referred to above has a most complicated amatory inscription both inside and outside, enclosing the message of love in a grammatical metaphor. On the outside appear the words '*une fame nominative a fait de moy son datiff par la parole genitive en depit de lacusatiff*'; and inside, next to the lady with the squirrel, '*srs amour est infiniti[v]e ge veu son relatiff*' (A nominative lady has made me her dative by the genitive word despite the accusative – love is infinitive for her relative). The meaning of this is that the ring has been given to a named lady as a possession despite her opposition – her lover has infinite love for her. Such secret and symbolic expressions of love, which occur

90 Shield of Parade. Flemish, fifteenth century.

90, back cover

in the later part of the Middle Ages, developed from the ideals of love expressed earlier in literary form by the troubadour poets.

In contrast to symbolic expressions of love, an often reproduced illustration of courtly love of the end of the Middle Ages occurs on the Flemish Shield of Parade. This shield is quite decoratively painted and would never have seen the field of war. It was probably a gift or a prize in a tournament. Jewels were certainly given as tournament prizes: for instance, Philip the Good, Duke of Burgundy, gave a jewel in the shape of a golden swan with a golden chain as a prize at a tournament held in Lille in 1454.

On the two sides of the long shield are three skilfully painted figures. On the left stands a young lady dressed in rich brocade trimmed with fur. She wears a high henin, an elaborate pointed Flemish headdress, from which lace falls. Around her waist is a gold chain which she holds in both hands. She looks down towards a man in armour who is arising from kneeling before her. His left arm is raised, his right dropped beside him. He is wearing a sword suitable for the tournament and in front of him are placed his helmet, gauntlets and pole-axe. Behind him stands a figure of death with a skull for a head, who extends both hands towards the man in armour. Above is a band on which there is the motto '*vous ou la mort*' (you or death). The armed man is about to take part in a tournament in order to win the lady's love but in which he fears death will win his life. Perhaps he is using the threat of his death to sway his lady to pity him. Alternatively, it could mean that Death, destroyer of the young and beautiful, is about to capture this young man.

This is a far cry from the gaiety and abandon with which the young ladies in the Castle of Love pelt their assailants with roses. Medieval art shows many different attitudes to love, though it is questionable how far these artistic representations reflected the wide range of people's thoughts and feelings. Much recent work has concentrated on the dating, manufacture and use of medieval objects, but their decoration, particularly the subjects chosen, has received less attention. It is only through looking at and studying the surviving fragments of secular art that we may come to appreciate the richness and complexity of medieval life.

Further reading

The best general bibliography on this subject is to be found in *Age of Chivalry: Art in Plantagenet England 1200–1400*, ed. J. Alexander and P. Binski, Royal Academy, 1987. Other general works are Joan Evans, *Pattern: A Study of Ornament in Western Europe from 1180 to 1900*, 1931, vol.I, and *London Museum Medieval Catalogue*, ed. J. B. Ward Perkins, 1940.

NATURE AND RURAL LIFE

N. Pevsner, *Leaves of Southwell*, 1945.

M. Remnant and R. Marks, 'A medieval gittern', *British Museum Yearbook*, 4, 1979, pp.83–134.

R. Camber and J. Cherry, 'The Savernake Horn', *British Museum Yearbook*, 2, 1977, pp.201–11.

K. Varty, *Reynard the Fox*, 1967.

H. W. Janson, *Apes and Ape Lore in the Middle Ages and the Renaissance*, 1952.

F. Klingender, *Animals in Art and Thought*, 1971.

M. Jones, 'Folklore motifs in late medieval art I: Proverbial follies and impossibilities', *Folklore*, vol.100:ii, 1989, pp.201–15.

G. E. Hutchinson, 'Attitudes towards nature in medieval England: The Alphonso and Bird psalters', *Isis*, vol.65, 1974, pp.5–37.

HERALDRY AS DECORATION

British Heraldry, ed. R. Marks and A. Payne, 1978.

W. H. St John Hope, *Heraldry for Craftsmen and Designers*, 1913.

T. Woodcock, *The Oxford Guide to Heraldry*, 1988.

J. H. Harvey, 'The Wilton Diptych: A re-examination', *Archaeologia*, XCVII, 1961, pp.1–28.

FEASTING

M. Wood, *The English Medieval House*, 1965.

B. Henisch, *Fast and Feast: Food in medieval society*, 1976.

J. Backhouse, *The Luttrell Psalter*, 1989.

M. Camille, 'Labouring for the Lord: The ploughman and the social order in the Luttrell psalter', *Art History*, X, no.4 (1987), pp.423–54.

ROMANCE AND COURTLY LOVE

D. D. R. Owen, *Noble Lovers*, 1975.

R. S. Loomis, *Arthurian Legends in Medieval Art*, 1938.

R. S. Loomis, *Illustrations of Medieval Romance on Tiles from Chertsey Abbey*, 1916.

E. Eames, *English Medieval Tiles*, 1985.

E. Eames, *Catalogue of Medieval Lead-glazed Earthenware Tiles in the British Museum*, 1980.

J. Cherry, 'Medieval rings' in A. Ward, J. Cherry, C. Gere and B. Cartlidge, *The Ring*, 1981.

M. Jones, 'Folklore motifs in medieval art II: Sexist satire and popular punishments', *Folklore*, vol.101:i, 1990.

Places to visit

Medieval secular art can be seen in London in the displays of the Victoria and Albert Museum and the Museum of London. Medieval manuscripts can be seen in the galleries of the British Library. In London the Abbey (nave and royal tombs) and the Chapter House (tiled floor) at Westminster can be visited. Many local museums have displays of medieval pottery, but the following have particularly good displays of medieval secular objects: Grosvenor Museum Chester, Dorchester Museum, Lincoln, Norwich, Ashmolean Museum Oxford, Salisbury, and York. The Burrell Collection in Glasgow is strong in medieval secular art. English Heritage (EH) and the National Trust (NT) preserve a number of castles and houses where some of the original architectural setting of medieval secular art can be appreciated. In many cases the visitor must be careful to distinguish the medieval from the post-medieval additions or restorations. Further details can be obtained from English Heritage, Fortress House, 23 Savile Row, London W1X 2HE, or from the National Trust, 36 Queen Anne's Gate, London SW1H 9AS.

Cambridgeshire Longthorpe Tower (EH)
Cornwall Cothele (NT)
Derbyshire Haddon Hall (privately owned)
Devon Bradley Manor (NT) Kirkham House, Paignton (EH)
Essex Paycockes Coggeshall (NT)
Hants Merchants House, 58 French St, Southampton (EH)
Kent Igtham Mote (NT) Old Soar Manor, Plaxtol (EH) Penshurst Place (privately owned)
Lincs Gainsborough Old Hall (EH)
Northumberland Warkworth Castle (EH)
Oxfordshire Minster Lovell Hall (EH)
Shropshire Stokesay Castle (EH)
Sussex Alfriston Clergy House (NT)
Yorkshire Middleham Castle (EH) Wharram Percy village (EH)

Acknowledgements

I would like to acknowledge the help of the following: Marian Campbell, Malcolm Jones, Brian Spencer and Neil Stratford have commented on the text and supplied photographs. Mr. J. M. Wilkinson, whom I have never met, provided an initial challenge, Bridget Cherry encouraged me, and Nina Shandloff was most helpful in the final editing.

All objects are in the Department of Medieval and Later Antiquities and the copyright of the photographs belongs to the Trustees of the British Museum, unless stated otherwise.

Inside front cover 1974,10–1,1.
Title page 1841,6–24,1.
Contents page, 6 and 11 1963, 10–2,1.
1 Drawing reproduced from R. S. Loomis, *Arthurian Legends in Medieval Art* (1938), frontispiece.
2 1870,8–11,1.
3 Gray Art Gallery and Museum, Borough of Hartlepool HAPMG. 124.'86.
4 1898,5–21,1.
5 Capitals on SE side of Southwell Chapter house (photo J. Cherry).
7 Eames design no.522.
8 Longthorpe Tower interior. Courtauld Institute, reproduced by courtesy of E. C. Rouse.
9 1855,6–25,15. Drawn by Hans Rashbrook.
10 Seal attached to Add.Ch.11296. Board of the British Library.
12, 13 and 14 1975,4–1,1.
15 1987,1–3,1.
16 Tracing by S. W. Tracey. Society of Antiquaries of London.
17 1856,7–1,2242.
18 QCP 005,006,105,106.
19 1856,7–1,1665.
20 Cambridge University Library Ms Ii.4.26. By permission of the Syndics of Cambridge University Library.
21 Eames design no.1897.
22 Eames design no.1329.
23 The Burrell Collection, Glasgow Museums and Art Gallery. 46.56.
24 Reproduced by permission of the Musée des Arts Decoratifs, Paris.
25 Watercolour of the knives and sheath BM MLA 1855,12–1,118 by C. Praetorius in the Society of Antiquaries of London.
26 Ivory cat.102.
27 1856,6–19,1.
28 1888,6–8,8; OA 2132; 1877,1–16,19; 1947,10–7,1.
29 British Library Add. Mss 42130, fol.202b. Reproduced by courtesy of the Board of the British Library.
30 Eames designs nos.468 (Richard) and 467 (Saladin).
31 Obverse 1856,4–28,1; Reverse 1842 no.8.
32 1872,12–16,1.
33 BM CM 1915,5–7,573.
34 1880,3–10,1.
35 V&A 4–1865. Reproduced by courtesy of the Trustees of the Victoria and Albert Museum.
36 Reproduced by courtesy of the Warden and Fellows of All Souls College, Oxford.
37 Sloane Collection.
38 OA 100. Drawn by N. Griffiths.
39 60,5–19,1.
40 1966,7–3,1.
41 National Gallery, London, 4451. Reproduced by courtesy of the National Gallery.
42 1933,3–8,3.
43 Eames designs nos.1482–5.
44 1922,5–11,1.
45 British Library Royal Mss 14 E IV fol.244b.
46 British Library Add. Mss 42130 fol.208. Both reproduced by courtesy of the Board of the British Library.
47 Rubbing of the brass of Robert Braunche in St Margaret's, Kings Lynn, Norfolk.
48 Reproduced by permission of the Rector and Parochial Church Council of Lacock, Wiltshire.
49 1878,11–1,11 and 12.
50 1975,10–1,1.
51 1853,3–15,1.
52 1862,7–17,3.
53 1956,7–2,1.

Index

Figures in bold italics refer to illustrations